ASHE Higher Education Report: Volume 36, Number 4
Kelly Ward, Lisa E. Wolf-Wendel, Series Editors

Understanding the New Majority of Non-Tenure-Track Faculty in Higher Education: Demographics, Experiences, and Plans of Action

Adrianna Kezar

Cecile Sam

D1714848

Understanding the New Majority of Non-Tenure-Track Faculty in Higher Education: Demographics, Experiences, and Plans of Action
Adrianna Kezar and Cecile Sam
ASHE Higher Education Report: Volume 36, Number 4
Kelly Ward, Lisa E. Wolf-Wendel, Series Editors

ISSN 1551-6970   electronic ISSN 1554-6306   ISBN 978-1-1180-0266-7

The ASHE Higher Education Report is part of the Jossey-Bass Higher and Adult Education Series and is published six times a year by Wiley Subscription Services, Inc., A Wiley Company, at Jossey-Bass, 989 Market Street, San Francisco, California 94103-1741.

For subscription information, see the Back Issue/Subscription Order Form in the back of this volume.

CALL FOR PROPOSALS: Prospective authors are strongly encouraged to contact Kelly Ward (kaward@wsu.edu) or Lisa Wolf-Wendel (lwolf@ku.edu). See "About the ASHE Higher Education Report Series" in the back of this volume.

Visit the Jossey-Bass Web site at **www.josseybass.com.**

Printed in the United States of America on acid-free recycled paper.

The ASHE Higher Education Report is indexed in CIJE: Current Index to Journals in Education (ERIC), Current Abstracts (EBSCO), Education Index/Abstracts (H.W. Wilson), ERIC Database (Education Resources Information Center), Higher Education Abstracts (Claremont Graduate University), IBR & IBZ: International Bibliographies of Periodical Literature (K.G. Saur), and Resources in Education (ERIC).

Advisory Board

The ASHE Higher Education Report Series is sponsored by the Association for the Study of Higher Education (ASHE), which provides an editorial advisory board of ASHE members.

Contents

Executive Summary

The American faculty is changing. Tenure-track appointments that were once the majority employment type are no longer the established norm of higher education; approximately 65 percent of all new faculty appointments are now nontenure track. Part-time non-tenure-track faculty appointments now make up the bulk of that percentage. Despite these changes, many higher education institutions still operate as though non-tenure-track faculty are a supplementary workforce, while the percentage of non-tenure-track faculty continues to grow.

With the growing majority of non-tenure-track faculty, questions arise. Who are these faculty? What are their experiences? What does this faculty mean for undergraduate instruction and students? What is the role of tenure in higher education? How did higher education attain this majority of non-tenure-track faculty? Where does higher education go from here?

This monograph reviews and synthesizes the research on non-tenure-track faculty, and much of the research available looks to answer these questions. The research focuses on the demographics of non-tenure-track faculty, differences by discipline and institutional types, historical developments, non-tenure-track faculty experiences, and non-tenure-track faculty experiences and outcomes compared with tenured or tenure-track faculty.

The monograph also explores various plans of action and promising practices to incorporate non-tenure-track faculty into higher education institutions. Academic unions, professional groups, and scholars have recommended numerous solutions, but few have actually been implemented on campuses, for the most part leaving tenured and tenure-track faculty out of the process.

The authors also review a bottom-up approach to the plans of action that includes faculty leadership and is grounded in specific institutional contexts. These action plans are meant to complement plans led from the top down.

One of the goals of this monograph is to advance the current dialogue about the role of non-tenure-track faculty in higher education and the next steps toward the future of the faculty. The authors compare empirical data with the preconceived notions, ideologies, and anecdotal evidence to challenge stereotypes and misconceptions that people may have of non-tenure-track faculty, their quality, and their experience.

Some of the major themes and recommendations that form the foundation on which this monograph is based are as follows:

Non-tenure-track faculty are a heterogeneous mixture of people who differ greatly in terms of employment, experiences, job descriptions, and motivations. Reliable institutional, state, and national data are needed about non-tenure-track faculty. A systematic national dataset needs to be designed with all types of faculty in mind. With the ending of the National Studies of Postsecondary Faculty (NSOPF), it is important to have a continuing source of data that examine and categorize non-tenure-track faculty. Institutions need to establish more robust systems internally to collect information about non-tenure-track faculty, particularly differences by contract and discipline. Further studies on non-tenure-track faculty should also take into consideration the different functional typologies of non-tenure-track faculty and find ways of incorporating them into their samples as well as interpreting the data.

Non-tenure-track faculty currently account for a majority of the faculty in higher education. If the past thirty years are any indication of a trend, they will continue to play a large role in institutions of higher education. Nevertheless, most institutions have failed to incorporate long-term policies for non-tenure-track faculty. Stakeholders in institutions of higher education need to develop long-term strategies regarding non-tenure-track faculty, depending on the context of the institutions. Issues such as hiring practices, reappointment, compensation, benefits, work responsibilities, governance, and promotion should be addressed explicitly in an overall institutional faculty plan and carried out consistently.

The research on non-tenure-track faculty could be theorized in more meaningful ways to best capture the faculty experience as a hybrid of professional and laborer. Research can apply theories from other disciplines such as political science or organizational studies to further explore the role of non-tenure-track faculty and their effect on higher education. Researchers can better understand non-tenure-track faculty by using a multidisciplinary perspective that incorporates insights from economics, sociology, psychology, and labor relations.

Misconceptions and stereotypes about non-tenure-track faculty, whether positive or negative, do not serve the population well because they do not provide accurate information that is needed to inform policies and practices that benefit both the faculty and the institution. Studies that move away from a deficit perspective can provide us a new way of understanding non-tenure-track faculty and enhance our knowledge. Studies should examine the positive features of the non-tenure-track faculty experience such as love of teaching, program environment, appreciation for academia, work with students, service to society, and fulfillment of personal priorities. Instead of ideology, empirical data about non-tenure-track faculty should drive policy and practice. These data include evidence suggesting that they lack basic necessities to complete their work, are as committed as tenure-track faculty, and are not paid for office hours at most institutions.

Many recommendations for improving working conditions for non-tenure-track faculty have been highly generalized and have not examined site-specific changes needed in programs, departments, colleges, and universities. Although global plans and ideas for professionalizing non-tenure-track faculty have been extremely helpful, they also have masked important variations that leaders should take into consideration as they institutionalize change. To move forward, solutions need to take into account the institutional context and different typology of non-tenure-track faculty to provide solutions that better serve different groups in different institutions. It is necessary to inform other institutions through more case study research and examples of institutions that have altered their policies and practices.

This monograph provides a needed synthesis of the existing literature and advice for practitioners trying to define policies and practices for non-tenure track faculty, policymakers attempting to understand the empirical research available to inform their decisions, and researchers seeking to conduct research on non-tenure-track faculty.

Given the large amount of data that must be synthesized to develop an accurate portrait, the authors expand on the topic of non-tenure track faculty with a follow-up issue of ASHE Higher Education Report, in connection with this monograph. Volume 36, issue number 5, "Non-Tenure-Track Faculty in Higher Education: Theories and Tensions," (referenced in upcoming chapters) builds on the research featured in this monograph and focuses on theories applied to study non-tenure-track faculty and philosophical and practical tensions represented in the literature.

Foreword

There is some discussion in the field about what to call non-tenure-track faculty. Labels are important, and non-tenure-track faculty have earned many different labels—contingent faculty, adjuncts, lecturers, instructors, clinical faculty, and part-timers. Understanding the distinction between the term "non-tenure-track" faculty (used in this monograph) and "contingent" faculty is especially illuminating. According to *Webster's* dictionary, "contingent" is an adjective that means "likely but not certain to happen" or "a happening by chance or unforeseen causes." So a contingent faculty member is someone whose labor may or may not be needed by the institution and who may or may not be employed at any one time. In other words, a contingent faculty member is someone who works at the pleasure of an institution, school, or department according to their ever-changing needs. This description is probably very accurate, although it obscures important differences in the group. Because of variations in the groups, for example, much of what one has to say about part-time faculty is not applicable to full-time non-tenure-track faculty and vice versa. Institutional and departmental differences also become important distinctions. Still, the term "non-tenure-track" is problematic, because it defines a group of individuals by what they are not—tenured or eligible for tenure. Although no good resolution to this question of labels is available, it is important to know that this group of faculty represent the majority of U.S. faculty today. By some estimates, 70 percent of the current faculty in the United States and the vast majority of new hires are nontenure track—and thus contingent faculty. This situation has led the American Association of University Professors to suggest that although "the tenure track has not vanished, it has ceased to be the norm." Some might even describe non-tenure-track faculty as the "new normal."

This new normal is the focus of the present monograph. The monograph clearly and carefully helps the reader to understand the complexity of the characterization of non-tenure-track faculty in all its conceptual messiness. The timeliness of the monograph is reflected in a recent call to action by the Coalition of Contingent Academic Labor and the American Association of University Professors. Both groups recently endorsed a plan to provide some form of "tenure-like rights" (if not tenure itself) for non-tenure-track faculty. The proposed plan, which may be more of a vision statement than an actual plan, argues that institutions of higher education should no longer treat non-tenure-track faculty as second-class citizens but should provide job security, academic freedom, and the other rights and privileges that come with tenure. Citing the inequity of having a two-class system of academics, other groups and individuals have called for the elimination of non-tenure-track appointments (which is not likely) or the elimination of tenure for those who have it (moving to an all-contingent instructional workforce). The either/or nature of these proposals as a means of bringing about equity in the academic profession lacks nuance and shows how important it is for everyone involved in the academic profession (including policymakers) to understand the forces at work that have brought us to where we are today. Such polarized suggestions underscore the importance and need for a monograph on this topic.

This monograph reviews all the major publications on the topic but builds specifically on the foundation established by Gappa and Leslie (1993), whose research on part-time faculty established the baseline for what we know about this part of the contingent faculty population. It also builds on the work of Baldwin and Chronister (2001), whose focus is full-time non-tenure-track faculty. With these pieces as a foundation, the monograph offers institutional decision makers a much-needed understanding of the experiences of non-tenure-track faculty along with their impact on the institution and on students. Most important, the monograph informs campus discussions by unmasking stereotypes and misconceptions of non-tenure-track faculty and making ideological and practical tensions between tenure-track and contingent faculty more apparent. The monograph also reframes the decision to create non-tenure-track appointments into broader decisions about campus staffing and eliminates the either/or propositions suggested earlier.

We have experienced fundamental shifts in the nature of the professoriate in ways that affect every aspect of postsecondary education. It is time to understand more about what that shift is, how it has occurred, its impact, and the future of the professoriate. This monograph offers an important glimpse into these issues in a thoughtful, provocative, and important way. I hope you gain as much from this monograph as I have and come to understand why it is a topic to which we are devoting two consecutive issues.

Lisa E. Wolf-Wendel
Series Editor

Published online in Wiley Online Library
(wileyonlinelibrary.com) • DOI: 10.1002/aehe.3604

Introduction and Overview

> Academic tenure is too prevalent a practice to disappear and too
> consequential a policy to disregard.
>
> —Chait and Ford, 1982, ix

THESE WORDS ARE NOW QUITE IRONIC in a world where tenure
has been in significant decline and the workforce is changing to a largely
non-tenure-track faculty. The shift in the composition of faculty has received
limited attention until recently.[1] In the last five years, a few books have documented this demographic shift, most prominently Schuster and Finkelstein's
The American Faculty: The Restructuring of Academic Work and Careers (2006).
Although early books tried to bring visibility to part-time and full-time non-
tenure-track faculty, who were largely ignored in the academy, these books
were developed before the increase in part-time numbers and rise of full-time
non-tenure-track faculty (Gappa and Leslie, 1993; Baldwin and Chronister,
2001). Through these initial texts as well as greater awareness on individual
campuses, people are beginning to recognize the major change in faculty composition that has taken place. We know little, however, about the implications
of this change. Several researchers who have analyzed or explored non-tenure-
track faculty have done so from focused perspectives, examining the growing
numbers (Schuster and Finkelstein, 2006; Gappa and Leslie, 1993; Baldwin
and Chronister, 2001; Hollenshead and others, 2007), the reasons for the
growth in non-tenure-track faculty (Cross and Goldenberg, 2003), or
the experience of being a non-tenure-track faculty member (Baldwin and
Chronister, 2001; Gappa and Leslie; 1993, Schell and Stock, 2001). A few

texts take a comprehensive view (Gappa and Leslie, 1993, and Baldwin an Chronister, 2001, are the major exceptions) and examine a plethora of topic: the reasons for growth, the expectations of non-tenure-track faculty, the natur of work role and career trajectories, and policies and practices institutions ca implement that can improve the working conditions for non-tenure-track fac ulty. Furthermore, because the landscape is changing rapidly, these texts ar becoming outdated. We build on these two important texts by examining ne research on the effect of non-tenure-track faculty on the academy, discussin rising tensions in the empirical research, and synthesizing the significar empirical literature to date.

Need for the Monograph

Much of the literature about non-tenure-track faculty has been ideologicall driven and attempts to either portray these faculty as destroying the integrit of the academic environment and threatening tenure or to demonstrate th oppression of the faculty experience and demonstrate how non-tenure-trac faculty represent the inequities and problems of the academy. Certainly excep tions exist such as the data-driven work by Schuster and Finkelstein (2006 Baldwin and Chronister (2001) and Gappa and Leslie (1993). This mone graph takes a more balanced approach, looking at the pros and cons and a the complexities of the lives of non-tenure-track faculty and the implicatior of this workforce for the academy. A more balanced and holistic perspectiv helps policymakers and campus leaders to make better decisions about the campuses. We present all perspectives, as no book so far has brought togethe both ideological and data-driven perspectives in one place.

Moreover, because of the nature of empirical research and the specificit that it requires, it is difficult to obtain a bird's-eye view of non-tenure-trac faculty. Many of the texts on non-tenure-track faculty focus only on part-tim faculty (Gappa and Leslie, 1993) or only on full-time non-tenure-track fac ulty (Baldwin and Chronister, 2001). Much of the literature also does not rec ognize disciplinary differences or differences by institutional type. The workin conditions, policies, solutions, and experience of non-tenure-track faculty var vastly by work status (part time or full time), discipline, and institutional typ

Furthermore, the presence of unions on campus also makes a difference in the experiences and working conditions of faculty. This monograph is sensitive to these types of differences that are often overlooked or fragmented in the literature.

Why is understanding non-tenure-track faculty so important? They are the most common appointments, with three out of every four being off the tenure track—part and full time (Schuster and Finkelstein, 2006; Forrest Cataldi, Fahimi, and Bradburn, 2005). Certainly their sheer numbers suggest that we need to understand more about them and their impact on the academy. More important, the main contribution of this monograph and reason for exploring non-tenure-track faculty is that we can no longer continue to operate according to the *perceived* status quo, pretending that tenured faculty are the mainline faculty of the academy. This reality has come to pass in the last twenty years, and campus leaders, faculty, staff, students, policymakers, and the general public should realize that we need more intentional planning and analysis of this new workforce—or, as some suggest, we need to revisit the value of tenure. Will we make the non-tenure-track faculty route a professional, recognized, and rewarding career option? Will we revisit faculty roles more generally?

Many campuses across the country have done little to change their policies and practices to acknowledge and professionalize the non-tenure-track faculty. Campuses lack a general awareness of the large growth of numbers. Those campuses that are slowly becoming aware of the growth are struggling to understand new policies and practices that can be put in place (and have long and extended campus discussions about whether *any* should be put in place). The most important reason for understanding and examining non-tenure-track faculty, however, is that they teach the majority of students in higher education; thus, they are key to creating the teaching and learning environment. They are in large measure the individuals responsible for meeting the primary mission of postsecondary institutions, and to know so little about who these faculty are (and how to support them) is at best reckless and at worst unethical. Faculty work conditions, many argue, are related to student learning conditions (Benjamin, 2002, 2003a, 2003b; Kezar and Sam, 2009; Curtis and Jacobe, 2006; Umbach, 2007). Understanding the experience and impact of non-tenure-track faculty is important to identify policies needed to refashion the academy. A fundamental change in the workforce has occurred, but understanding of this shift is limited.

Purpose and Audience

Our overarching goal in this monograph is to fill the void in the literature that lacks a meta-analysis of the research about non-tenure-track faculty. The existing research is difficult to wade through; it is produced by many groups with differing agendas and focused on varying goals and facets of the non-tenure-track issue. Thus, our first goal is to synthesize and analyze the research that is available to provide the reader a better understanding of this new majority. Another major purpose of meta-analysis is to critique the literature and to help find new directions for research and practice. In reviewing the research on non-tenure-track faculty, we realized that they have been conceptualized and theorized in limited ways (see Kezar and Sam, 2010b). Our second goal is to offer new approaches for conceptualizing and researching non-tenure-track faculty. The review of research also made misconceptions and misinterpretations of non-tenure-track faculty, often based on faulty underlying assumptions, prominent. Our third goal is to offer some recommendations so that campuses can create better policies and practices and policymakers can make important decisions related to non-tenure-track faculty. By having a comprehensive source of the research and literature on non-tenure-track faculty, we hope to lay down the foundation for reasoned, intelligent, and ethical dialogue among stakeholders in the academy that will lead to changing the status quo that currently is not serving students or the general public.

The ASHE Series aims to serve practitioners by creating syntheses of research that are readable and largely nontechnical so that campus administrators can use the work to inform their decisions. Although all the chapters contain data that can help inform campus policy, "Plans of Action and Promising Policies" (in this monograph) has ideas that administrators and non-tenure-track faculty can use to address the working conditions of non-tenure-track faculty. The other chapters explaining the changing nature of non-tenure-track faculty, experience of non-tenure-track faculty, and even theories used to understand non-tenure-track faculty inform the plans of action and conclusions and are critical logic that administrators will need to support their policies. The other major audience for this monograph is researchers studying non-tenure-track faculty. A synthesis of research develops a clear direction for future research. As noted earlier, our meta-analysis critiques faulty and problematic assumptions and methodologies that can help improve future research. This monograph also helps identify key gaps in our knowledge that help determine new directions for study.

Terminology

We refer to this growing new profile of faculty as *nontenure track* for both part-time and full-time appointments that are ineligible for tenure review. We believe it is important to have an umbrella term to refer to this large population and to examine some similarities individuals off the tenure track share. We acknowledge that using only the term *non-tenure-track faculty* to describe the entire population of faculty not on the tenure track lacks precision, as members of this group vary tremendously. One major difference referred to in the literature is part time versus full time. We refer to part-time and full-time non-tenure-track faculty throughout the monograph to point out important differences in these groups, but we point out that the plethora of terms that have emerged have caused tremendous confusion, and we avoid using the alphabet soup of names that have emerged: contingent, lecturer, instructor, clinical faculty, adjunct, and more. Terminology is one of the most difficult conundrums of recognizing and understanding non-tenure-track faculty. Most terms for this group of faculty reflect a particular element of focus (lecturer) that they teach or amount of teaching (part time), but these terms do not comprehensively reflect their status. Given the vast number of names in the literature, we wanted some clear terminology to break this confusion; thus, our umbrella term when we refer to similarities these groups share is "nontenure track." When meaningful differences exist, they usually reflect the part-time and full-time contract status, so we use these two terms when they are relevant to identify significant differences in these groups.

Although we use the term *nontenure track,* other groups have gravitated toward the word *contingent* because it reflects the precarious nature of the contracts of part-time and full-time non-tenure-track faculty (the National Education Association and the American Federation of Teachers, for example). Others have recommended the label *lecturer,* because being defined as what a faculty member is not—tenure track—seems problematic as well. Even among the faculty, conflicts exist related to terminology, with some terms being more preferred than others. For example, some faculty find the word "adjunct" to describe faculty who teach part time distasteful, while others do not mind. We recognize that these terms are value laden and problematic. The evolution of these terms is hard to trace, but what is important to understand is that more than fifty terms exist for non-tenure-track faculty and that in recent years an effort has been made to narrow the terminology and to come up with more precise and standard terminology. We follow this practice of standardizing language in this monograph while respecting a major difference in employment—full and part time.

Although we need some term to refer to this growing group of faculty—in our case *nontenure track*—we are clear throughout the monograph to break out studies and research specific to part-time and full-time non-tenure-track faculty when such a designation is made. Many studies have not broken down the research and disaggregated these groups, but when studies are specific to these populations, we note this information. We seek to make the trends about full-time and part-time faculty clear to readers, but because many researchers have not studied these groups separately, we are not always able to make these distinctions. It is important to note that part-time faculty are represented more in community colleges and in certain disciplines such as law. Full-time non-tenure-track faculty are represented more in four-year institutions and in certain disciplines such as mathematics. We review these types of statistics in more detail in future chapters, but it is important to note that non-tenure-track faculty are shaped by institutional type and discipline. These structures play a major role in the experiences, commitment, and plans of action of non-tenure-track faculty.

It is important to note one methodological issue, also related to terminology. Some of the studies we report on focus only on part-time non-tenure-track faculty. When we report this data, we use the term "part-time" rather than "nontenure track" to make the reader understand that the study was limited to a subsection of non-tenure-track faculty. Other studies have looked exclusively at full-time non-tenure-track faculty, and another set of studies does not differentiate the two but has grouped together part time and full time or is unclear about the exact population. Less than one-tenth of part-time faculty have tenure; these groups have not been studied separately and are usually included with part-time track faculty. Where we have clarity, we make specific note; otherwise, we use the generic term to refer to non-tenure-track part-time faculty.

We would like to remind readers that, first and foremost, we are talking about faculty in higher education. We call people back to referring to all faculty as "the faculty." Making the majority of faculty take on a potentially negative or misleading label in the long run is likely to create more problems. In the short run, we do need to understand that the faculty is an incredibly diverse group with many different contracts currently, and we need to better understand the current distinctions so we can develop the best staffing arrangements for different campuses and institutions. But ultimately we argue that it is in the best interests of higher education to conceptualize the faculty as a single and united group, even if individual members of the group have different contracts.

Related to the notion of returning to a single term for the faculty, we also think it is important to think about the non-tenure-track faculty as part of the larger issue of defining the profession of faculty or staffing and human resources for higher education. It may be that people are reluctant to think about faculty hiring as a staffing or human resource issue because that term is associated with administrative actions and behavior. For those more comfortable with the term "profession" than "human resources," it is critical that faculty take more responsibility for who is part of the profession, who is teaching courses, who is creating a learning environment for students, and what it means to be a scholar, academic, and faculty member. Because tenure-track faculty have largely abdicated their role in defining the professoriate (some might argue that hiring decisions were taken away from the faculty during the corporatization of higher education), non-tenure-track faculty float along without a professional anchor or career route (Burgan, 2006). In the absence of the tenure-track faculty's defining what it means to be a professional without tenure, administrators have claimed this space, providing new types of contracts but minimal policies and procedures. But in large measure, few faculty or administrators have been thinking intentionally about bringing non-tenure-track faculty into the faculty profession and how they fit into the larger human resource and staffing arrangements for higher education. Our point is not to take sides about whether this is an issue of professionalization or academic staffing but to suggest that the question of non-tenure-track faculty is likely one that is best made in relationship to thinking about total faculty/staffing for the campus.

Background: Understanding the Conflicting Research

Scholars and writers about non-tenure-track faculty agree on few issues, with the exceptions that non-tenure-track faculty now constitute two-thirds of the faculty (with non-tenure-track full-time faculty being one-third of full-time faculty) and that their numbers have been rising significantly in the last two decades. After that well-documented fact, research evidence about non-tenure-track faculty is mixed, and interpretations of data are often one-sided, not examining alternative explanations. In writing this monograph, we undertake a great challenge because several conditions make it very difficult to clearly understand the background, experience, and effect of non-tenure-track faculty. Simple questions like "Are non-tenure-track faculty satisfied?" result in complex answers with little agreement among studies. Why such a confused landscape? We suggest that five primary conditions make the study of non-tenure-track faculty complex: ideology, theory, data sources, heterogeneity of the group, and a historical and contextual view.

Ideology

Researchers studying or writing about non-tenure-track faculty have generally adopted two different ideologies. Scholars maintaining the first perspective focus on non-tenure-track faculty and the exploitation that occurs—low salaries, minimal benefits, and a lack of job security. Unions and non-tenure-track faculty generally hold this position. The same authors often believe that non-tenure-track faculty are a threat to tenure and traditional academic staffing arrangements. Scholars maintaining the second perspective focus on the non-tenure-track faculty path as allowing career flexibility, particularly for women, see it as a way to bring in expertise to the institution, and believe that it is important to improve the working conditions for these faculty as they that have grown in numbers. Administrators but also faculty who are disillusioned with tenure often hold this perspective. A third, less often mentioned perspective blends the two ideologies, acknowledging the exploitation of some and the choice of others. Some non-tenure-track faculty in certain fields (English composition, for example) are being exploited and at only some campuses. Other non-tenure-track faculty have chosen this route and view it as an alternative to tenure. For them, tenure is a less desirable option for various reasons, such as the overly long working hours to produce research for tenure and promotion, which is often inhospitable to faculty with families.

These deeply ingrained perspectives affect people's interpretation of the data and the way they write about non-tenure-track faculty. Different people look at the same data and arrive at different conclusions. This phenomenon is similar to other controversial issues such as climate change, where ideology can make understanding the data extremely difficult. Data need to be interpreted, and the lenses people bring sway their views. Contested issues often have more varied interpretations and make consensus difficult. As noted earlier, these perspectives are often related to one's position as a tenure-track or non-tenure-track faculty, administrator, or union member.

Theory

Another issue that affects our understanding of non-tenure-track faculty is the theories (or lack of theories) brought to bear. Much of the research conducted is atheoretical and does not draw on known concepts about labor markets, contingent labor, work motivation, and non-tenure-track professionals. When theory is used, it draws from only a few disciplines—economic theories, sociological theories, psychological theories, and labor relations theories (see Kezar and Sam, 2010b). In terms of economic theories, dual market, supply and demand, underemployment, risk taking, and social exchange have been applied, focusing on general patterns in the economy, workforce restructuring, or contracts (Cross and

Goldenberg, 2009; Ehrenberg and Zhang, 2004, 2005; Toutkoushian and Bellas, 2003; Umbach, 2007). Sociological theories of the political economy examine how academic capitalism has come to prevail on college campuses, making market logic more important than educational goals and resulting in the deprofessionalization and deskilling of faculty—losing their tenure status and becoming managed professionals under their non-tenure-track status (Rhoades, 1996). Psychological theories such as commitment theory, person-job fit, and faculty growth and development look more at how individuals make choices and variations in satisfaction and impact (Bland and others, 2006; Maynard and Joseph, 2008; O'Meara, Terosky, and Neumann, 2008). Labor relations studies examine the way faculty can mobilize to create changes in working conditions and the role of unions. Organizational theory has been used fewer times and more tacitly than other theories, though exceptions exist such as Gappa and Leslie's work (1993) examining organizational concepts. All these theories have important insights to offer, but typically studies have applied a single economic, sociological, or psychological lens. Like the understanding of climate change, understanding non-tenure-track faculty may require an interdisciplinary perspective that draws together these various conceptual lenses.

Lack of Meaningful Data

Various researchers have noted the difficulty in accessing meaningful data about non-tenure-track faculty (Chait and Ford, 1982; Cross and Goldenberg, 2009). Researchers point to the challenge of even identifying non-tenure-track faculty because the names and labels used for non-tenure-track faculty vary by institution. Published lists of titles demonstrate close to fifty different terms used to identify part-time non-tenure-track faculty alone (Berry, 2005). As a result, studies typically miss many of the faculty based only on identification and terminology. Moreover at the institutional level, many non-tenure-track faculty, especially part-time faculty, are hired by departments from semester to semester; thus, the statistics and data change so rapidly that it is difficult for institutional research offices to sort out how many and what type of non-tenure-track faculty are hired. In a study of ten elite research universities (Cross and Goldenberg, 2009), none of the institutions could easily come up with data about the non-tenure-track faculty. Some states have better sources of data about employment and contracts than others, making available data uneven and not comparable. But because institutional data are often inaccurate, state-level data likely lacks accuracy as well. At the federal level, the National Study of Postsecondary Faculty (NSOPF) was one of the best sources of data about non-tenure-track faculty, but the survey was originally designed with tenure-track faculty largely in mind and has not always captured the experience and background of non-tenure-track faculty as sharply.

Unfortunately, the National Center for Education Statistics has decided it will no longer fund the NSOPF database, limiting any further research on faculty. The last national survey was in 2004. The Higher Education Research Institute (HERI) at the University of California, Los Angeles, also conducts regular national faculty surveys, every three years. In 2007–2008, it added more questions to specifically explore the non-tenure-track faculty experience. Like NSOPF, the survey was originally designed for tenure-track faculty and is still largely targeted toward tenure-track faculty. The survey sample also contains few community colleges but has grown in number in the last two cycles. Moreover, the HERI database is proprietary, and access is limited to those with the ability to pay. With limited data sources, researchers often conduct local and individual studies with smaller samples that are more feasible, but results are difficult to generalize.

Heterogeneity

Another issue that makes interpretation and conclusions difficult is that non-tenure-track faculty are heterogeneous. Some studies have assumed that non-tenure-track faculty were a homogeneous group and conducted large-scale surveys, making generalizations across vastly different faculty with different motivations, experiences, contracts, working conditions, disciplinary backgrounds, and institutional types (Bland and others, 2006; Jacoby, 2006; Umbach, 2007; Jaeger and Eagan, 2009; Eagan and Jaeger, 2009; Banachowski, 1996). Our review of the research demonstrates that the heterogeneous nature of non-tenure-track faculty is extremely meaningful to understanding their experience. Only by examining and disaggregating non-tenure-track faculty into subgroups can we truly understand their satisfaction, experience, and potentially their impact on higher education.

Historical and Contextual Analysis

Historical and social forces also shape our understanding of non-tenure-track faculty; we can achieve greater understanding by looking at them in the broader context of higher education and the changes that have been occurring. We will discuss the history and rise of non-tenure-track faculty in more detail in the next chapter, "Portrait of Non-Tenure-Track Faculty," but it is important to recognize that certain historical markers can help us to understand how we ended up with the current staffing patterns and demonstrate ways that we might alter and create better professional circumstances for faculty. For example, the rapid rise in full-time non-tenure-track faculty happened just after higher education came under critical attack in the late 1980s for largely abandoning undergraduate education. Studies and reports demonstrated that teaching assistants, not tenure-track faculty, were teaching introductory courses, particularly at large institutions (Study Group on the Conditions of Excellence in Higher Education, 1985). National reports critiqued campuses for not focusing on undergraduate education, which policymakers and taxpayers felt was a priority. Tenured faculty did not offer to teach introductory courses or change the nature of their work, so campuses turned to non-tenure-track faculty instead of teaching assistants. The general public did not understand that these new faculty were not the same as tenure-track faculty, but the public did understand that they were not teaching assistants. These broader historical trends help us to comprehend how we might rethink our current approach to staffing.

Introduction to the Players: Groups Studying Non-Tenure-Track Faculty

To understand the landscape of non-tenure-track faculty, it helps to be introduced to various players who have written about and created policy related to non-tenure-track faculty. The first group to write about non-tenure-track faculty were higher education scholars such as Leslie, Kellams, and Gunne (1982), Gappa and Leslie (1993), Bowen and Schuster (1986), and other scholars documenting changes in community college in the 1970s. The studies largely examined the rising numbers, examined the experiences and motivations of non-tenure-track faculty, primarily part-time faculty, and pointed out how these faculty were largely invisible, even as their numbers were growing. The research often focused on community colleges, as the emergence of part-time faculty happened to a greater degree in these institutions early in the 1970s and 1980s.

The rise in full-time non-tenure-track positions happened later in the 1990s. The Faculty Forum on Roles and Rewards of the American Association for Higher Education (AAHE) was formed in the 1990s and began to address the issues of non-tenure-track faculty, the changing nature of tenure, and the changing faculty. The forum focused more on the issue of full-time non-tenure-track faculty at four-year institutions—the emerging issue in the 1990s among AAHE members. One of the major projects that emerged out of the forum, the New Pathways Project, looked at a variety of alternatives to tenured positions as currently conceptualized. Driven by research that demonstrated that women and faculty of color often found tenure-track positions unwelcoming, the forum explored other avenues such as teaching-only tenure-track lines or nontenured faculty positions. The forum was also responding to Boyer's *Scholarship Reconsidered: Priorities of the Professoriate* (1990), which raised concerns about the narrow ways that faculty scholarship and life have been conceived, trying to broaden the perspective of faculty on the tenure-track career, largely focused on research over teaching and pure research rather than applied research.

In the late 1990s, many other groups began to recognize the large numbers of non-tenure-track faculty in the academy and to see the rise as problematic (Schell and Stock, 2001). In particular, various disciplinary societies began to address and conduct research on non-tenure-track faculty (for example, the *2002 AHA–OAH Survey of Part-time and Adjunct Faculty* and the *2000 Report of the Ad Hoc Committee on Priorities and Problems of the American Philosophical Association*). Liberal arts disciplines with high numbers of non-tenure-track faculty were the most active, including composition and history. Several of the disciplinary societies began to work on policy statements related to the use of non-tenure-track faculty and established a coalition across several disciplines that have high concentrations of non-tenure-track faculty: the Coalition on the Academic Workforce (Schell and Stock, 2001). Surprisingly, many fields that have larger numbers of non-tenure-track faculty such as law, medicine, and education were not actively involved in advocating for or researching non-tenure-track faculty. One of the major differences noted in the literature between these groups is that non-tenure-track faculty in vocational and professional areas often have other employment and are not interested in full-time employment in the academy. The research emerging from the disciplines adds a new perspective because it is conducted by non-tenure-track faculty themselves. Other studies conducted by tenure-track faculty have sometimes been biased against non-tenure-track faculty or misunderstood their experience and working conditions (Kezar and Sam, 2010b).

During the mid- to late 1990s, unions began to recognize, write about, and research non-tenure-track faculty. The American Association of University Professors (AAUP), the National Education Association (NEA), and the American Federation of Teachers (AFT) developed subgroups to work on policy statements related to non-tenure-track faculty. Each organization developed a report based on research advocating for certain changes in policies and practices on campus (see, for example, *Standards of Good Practice in the Employment of Full-Time Non-Tenure-Track Faculty: Professionals and Colleagues* [AFT Higher Education, 2005]). The AFT recently published (American Federation of Teachers, 2010) a national survey of the experience and background of non-tenure-track faculty. The NEA conducted national focus groups with non-tenure-track faculty in 2008 and 2009 and plans a national survey in 2010. The unions also carried out smaller-scale research efforts in the early 2000s. In addition, state and regional union groups became prominent in California, Illinois, Massachusetts, and Wisconsin, creating listservs, Web sites, and resources to help mobilize and support non-tenure-track faculty.

As an alternative to unions, other professional groups have begun to emerge from a growing number of non-tenure-track faculty leaders. These groups help provide support for non-tenure-track faculty, especially those in states that are unable to unionize. For example, Adjunct Nation has produced a series of publications such as the *Adjunct Advocate* to help non-tenure-track faculty (with an emphasis on part-time faculty) deal with challenging working conditions and provide a space for both mobilization and an exchange of ideas. Another group, the New Faculty Majority, aims to create a unified front across all disciplines and groups and to provide a united voice when speaking to legislators and policymakers.

Some states have also engaged in research on non-tenure-track faculty based on reports of inequitable treatment. For example, the state of Illinois in 2005 conducted a study examining the use and deployment of non-tenure-track faculty and found that their working conditions were not equitable with other faculty. California and New Mexico have also conducted studies of non-tenure-track faculty to examine whether states should recommend or encourage institutional policies and practices to better serve non-tenure-track faculty. In the future, we imagine more states will conduct research on non-tenure-track faculty, as non-tenure-track faculty are appealing more to legislatures related to their working conditions because they feel that higher education administrators or policymakers have been unresponsive to their concerns.

Higher education associations have also conducted research on non-tenure-track faculty; for example, the Association of American Universities (AAU) conducted a study of major research universities and their deployment of non-tenure-track faculty (2001), examining baseline data and recommending some best practices related to the use of non-tenure-track faculty. The American Council on Education (ACE) developed a publication using national data describing the rising trend, background, and experience of non-tenure-track faculty (Anderson, 2002). But the national higher education organizations have conducted less research than expected for such a significant national topic.

Each of these groups has different vested interests, which affect the way they study and describe the experience, working conditions, deployment, and impact of non-tenure-track faculty. Even the language they use and the focus they take to study the issue suggest a different vested interest. The AAU (2005) and the ACE (1981), for example, focus on the deployment and best use of both full-time and part-time non-tenure-track faculty as part of an overall human resource scheme, flexibility, and cost savings. Non-tenure-track faculty are more likely to study the experience and working conditions of non-tenure-track faculty in an effort to demonstrate problems that they themselves have experienced. Each perspective sheds light on the issue, but similar to the theories, they tend to shine only partial light. Looking across the perspectives can help enhance our knowledge. These various groups also represent sources of bias in interpretation that need to be recognized as well.

Although we cannot pretend to be free of any perspective, our goal in reviewing the research has been to be open to differing perspectives and to present multiple views. Yet we acknowledge we hold some basic assumptions. Non-tenure-track faculty will likely be part of academic institutions in the future and in large numbers. Their current treatment at many institutions does not fall in line with best organizational practices. We think that there are ways to incorporate non-tenure-track faculty into the academy that can serve to strengthen higher education. Although we think that tenure is a valuable structure, it may not be desirable in all circumstances, and we think that tenure reforms should be debated and considered. Although our perspective may be apparent in some of our discussion, we hope that the meta-analysis reflects a range of views and helps people consider multiple alternatives.

Organization of the Monograph

In this monograph, we provide a portrait of non-tenure-track faculty, describe studies of their experiences, and propose plans of action.

Much of the research, particularly early on, tried to provide a picture and description of this faculty that have been largely invisible for years. Therefore, "Portrait of Non-Tenure-Track Faculty" focuses on the history and rise of non-tenure-track faculty, typologies developed to understand different non-tenure-track faculty, and demographic data and trends. The important insight offered through these data is the heterogeneity of this group of faculty in terms of the nature of their work and institutional contracts. In addition, it is important to understand that non-tenure-track faculty in the 1970s were largely part time and that now the trend has moved toward full-time non-tenure-track faculty.

"Experiences of Non-Tenure-Track Faculty" examines the research on the experience of non-tenure-track faculty, including the differentiation among different faculty groups. Although initial research helped us understand part-time versus full-time appointments, race, gender, educational background, and distribution by institution, later research began to examine the attitudes and perceptions of non-tenure-track faculty related to their jobs and working conditions, particularly their satisfaction in light of the emerging evidence of inequitable pay and benefits. The chapter also highlights research on improving policy and practices related to the working conditions of non-tenure-track faculty that followed from much of the research on their experiences.

"Plans of Action and Promising Policies" is based on the research presented in earlier chapters. It provides recommendations for rethinking faculty as a professional group and staffing arrangements in higher education. It also presents recommendations of specific groups such as policy documents created by the AFT (American Federation of Teachers, 2002, 2005) or researchers such as Gappa and Leslie (1993). Our approach toward change not only incorporates the top-down suggestions of other scholars but also a bottom-up approach to changing the academy. This chapter largely draws on a synthesis of research to inform directions forward. The final chapter offers conclusions related to research from earlier chapters and provides ideas for future research.

In the end, we are trying to address the important questions and their elusive answers, such as to what extent institutions should rely on non-tenure-track faculty, how colleges and universities can employ these individuals in a way that is fair to all faculty, how faculty can be organized so that it strengthens institutional capacity to meet their missions of teaching students and advancing knowledge, and how to address quality issues that emerge because of the change in faculty. As Schuster and Finkelstein (2006) note, a revolution has taken place in the faculty, and it would be irresponsible not to better understand this issue. Now that a body of research has been amassed, we have taken on the task of organizing and synthesizing this research to try to answer these questions and to propose future research that will help us address these questions.

Our meta-analysis relies heavily on three comprehensive studies: *The Invisible Faculty: Improving the Status of Part-Timers in Higher Education* (Gappa and Leslie, 1993) focused exclusively on part-time faculty; *Teaching Without Tenure* (Baldwin and Chronister, 2001) focused on full-time non-tenure-track faculty; and *Making the Best of Both Worlds* (Hollenshead and others, 2007), which is the only national study looking at all non-tenure-track faculty in four-year institutions. *The Invisible Faculty* is a qualitative case study of multiple institutions examining policies and practices related to part-time faculty—hiring, salary, benefits, governance. The authors interviewed administrators and tenure-track faculty about their views of part-time faculty and talked to part-time faculty about their experiences. *Teaching Without Tenure* is also a qualitative case study of multiple institutions examining policies and practices related to full-time non-tenure-track faculty. It was the first major study to focus on this growing population. The book ranges in topics from the history and reasons for growth to reports about policies and practices used on campuses to a report of the experiences of full-time non-tenure-track faculty. *Making the Best of Both Worlds* is a national quantitative study of approximately 500 institutions asking administrators about their deployment, policies, and practices relative to both part-time and full-time non-tenure-track faculty. It is one of the few studies to disaggregate these groups in studies and examine differences in policy.

In volume 36, issue number 5 of ASHE Higher Education Report, Kezar and Sam also cover other important topics focused on the theoretical underpinnings of non-tenure-track faculty, the practical and ideological tensions used to study non-tenure-track faculty, and advice for framing future research on non-tenure-track faculty.

Portrait of Non-Tenure-Track Faculty

> Historically, faculty off the tenure track have been viewed from a policy perspective as an academic equivalent of migrant workers.
>
> —Baldwin and Chronister, 2001, p. 155

AS WE EXPLORE THE RESEARCH on non-tenure-track faculty, it is important to gain an understanding of the people and their role in the higher education setting. As noted earlier, the types of non-tenure-track faculty are varied and numerous and, as we discuss later, so are their experiences. This chapter paints a portrait of non-tenure-track faculty to give readers a better understanding of the people in this workforce and to help them understand studies reported on in the next chapters. Similar to pointillist portraits, from afar non-tenure-track faculty can be understood in broad general terms as those faculty who are ineligible for tenure in their current appointment. Upon closer inspection, however, we see that the faculty comprises numerous, distinctly different types of non-tenure-track faculty, with distinctions ranging from work hours to responsibilities to motivations. Understanding these individual differences among the faculty becomes particularly important for those wanting to enact successful policy changes and those who seek to understand further non-tenure-track faculty and their work.

This chapter begins with the overall trends of non-tenure-track faculty, focusing on part-time and full-time faculty separately in terms of increases in the overall faculty, increases in particular institutional sectors, and increases in disciplines. Second, it explores the historical developments to establish the background that gave rise to the use of non-tenure-track faculty. Many of the relevant factors that occurred in the past are still very relevant. If trends in academia continue such as expanding enrollments and limited budgets, these factors will still be important in the future. Though many common reasons exist for the growth of non-tenure-track faculty, the trajectories of part-time and full-time appointments took varying paths. Next this chapter explores the various typologies and subsequent titles used to categorize and frame subgroups in this rising population of faculty. The typologies in many ways reflect the various ways that people conceptualize and understand non-tenure-track faculty, both in the past and present. The typologies also illustrate that, in some instances, a need exists to reframe those conceptualizations. For example, non-tenure-track faculty are often categorized as part time and full time based on either number of classes taught or instructional hours, and policies and practices are applied based on that distinction. It may be, however, that the distinction between part-time and full-time faculty is a less useful typology than the motivations of the faculty to be nontenure track when creating policy. Finally, this chapter reviews trends and data about non-tenure-track faculty, including demographic composition of non-tenure-track faculty, faculty degrees, and distinctions among institutional types. This chapter seeks to provide context, details, and definition to an otherwise "invisible faculty" (Gappa and Leslie, 1993).

Trends in Part-Time and Full-Time Non-Tenure-Track Faculty

The general data on non-tenure-track faculty over the last twenty-five years show an inverse relationship between the number of tenure- and non-tenure-track positions: as tenure-track positions diminish, non-tenure-track positions increase, according to the AAUP's *Non-Tenure-Track Faculty Index* (Curtis and Jacobe, 2006). Using data from the Integrated Postsecondary Education Data System (IPEDS), Curtis and Jacobe (2006) worked with a dataset consisting of 2,617 institutions and found that from 1975 to 2003, as the full-time tenured faculty diminished from 36.5 percent to 24.1 percent of the entire faculty population and as the full-time tenure-track faculty diminished from 20.3 percent to 11 percent, the number of full-time and part-time non-tenure-track faculty increased. From 1975–2003, full-time non-tenure-track faculty increased from 13 percent to 18.7 percent. However, the greatest increase in hires occurred among part-time non-tenure-track faculty, jumping from 30.2 percent to 46.3 percent by 2003, almost half the entire faculty population (Curtis and Jacobe, 2006).

Part-Time Faculty

Part-time faculty appointments have grown significantly since the 1970s. Schuster and Finkelstein (2006) note that part-time faculty increased by 376 percent, roughly five times faster than the rate of increase of full-time faculty (tenured and nontenured). In 1970 there were 104,000 part-time faculty and 369,000 full-time faculty; by 2003 there were 543,000 part-time faculty and 630,000 full-time faculty (Schuster and Finkelstein, 2006). It is important to note that included in this number of part-time faculty are those part-time faculty who also have tenure, but according to the NSOPF:03, part-time faculty with tenure accounted for 3 percent and those on the tenure track for only 1.5 percent of all part-time faculty—a small percentage of the overall number of part-time faculty[2] (Forrest Cataldi, Fahimi, and Bradburn, 2005).

Institutional differences. With regard to part-time faculty, Gappa and Leslie (1993) found differences among the different types of institutions. Community colleges seemed to have the greatest percentage of part-time faculty; in some schools they were the majority of faculty (Eagan, 2007; Gappa and Leslie, 1993). More recently, the percentage at some schools has been as high as 80 percent (National Education Association Research Center, 2007; American Federation of Teachers, 2003). Research and doctorate-granting universities have begun to follow the employment patterns of community colleges, with an increasing number of part-time faculty. According to a study by the AFT (American Federation of Teachers, 2009), from 1997 to 2007 the use of part-time faculty increased overall in all institutions. Community colleges increased their part-time faculty population from 65 percent to 69 percent. Public comprehensive institutions saw a growth of part-time faculty from 34 percent to 44 percent. Public research institutions saw a growth from 14 percent to 16 percent, but it is important to note that in these institutions the number of graduate assistants (higher than in all the institutions) grew from 37 percent to 41 percent. In 2003 part-time faculty accounted for 54.9 percent of the faculty in private not-for-profit master's institutions and 36.8 percent of faculty in private not-for-profit baccalaureate institutions (Forrest Cataldi, Fahimi, and Bradburn, 2005).

Academic fields. The prevalence of part-time faculty also varies based on the academic program. Programs with the highest percentage of part-time faculty appointments to overall faculty were education (48.7 percent), fine arts (47.0 percent), and business (46.0 percent). In the humanities, 34.6 percent of the faculty were part time, in health sciences 30.3 percent, social sciences 29.7 percent, natural sciences 23.5 percent, engineering 21.8 percent, and agriculture/home economics 21.6 percent (Forrest Cataldi, Fahimi, and Bradburn, 2005). Of other programs not included in the above lists, 37.4 percent of total faculty in those programs were part time. It is also important to look at where the largest growth or increase is occurring to understand where higher education is headed. According to a report by the National Education Association Research Center (2007), the highest increases in part-time faculty occurred in the humanities (13.2 percent), social sciences (15.4 percent), and agriculture (12.2 percent), with the greatest increase from 1987 to 2003 in education, which increased 27.7 percent over those years.

Full-Time Faculty

Unlike the part-time faculty population, the number of full-time non-tenure-track faculty did not increase significantly until the early 1990s. In 1993 a rise in the proportion of full-time non-tenure-track new appointments made them the majority of the full-time faculty hires. Tracking every two years thereafter until 2003, Schuster and Finkelstein (2006) found that non-tenure-track faculty continued to be the majority of new full-time appointments to such an extent that nontenure hires were the norm. By 2003, 58.6 percent of new full-time faculty hires were nontenure track (approximately 26,000 faculty hires), compared with the 37.4 percent of hires who were on the tenure track and the 4 percent who held tenure. The increase in new hires has changed the representation of full-time non-tenure-track faculty as a whole. Of the 630,000 full-time faculty in higher education by 2003, 219,000 (34.8 percent) were off the tenure track (Schuster and Finkelstein, 2006).

Institutional differences. Though the number of full-time non-tenure-track faculty increased throughout the various types of institutions, they are most notable among the four-year research universities and less common at baccalaureate institutions (Shavers, 2000). In 1969 full-time non-tenure-eligible faculty were 3.4 percent of full-time faculty; by 1998, 16.4 percent of full-time faculty were ineligible for tenure (Schuster and Finkelstein, 2006). In 2003 both public and private doctoral institutions had the highest percentage of full-time nontenured faculty compared with each full-time faculty population, with 30.3 percent and 32.7 percent, respectively (Forrest Cataldi, Fahimi, and Bradburn, 2005). At private master's and baccalaureate institutions, approximately 22 percent of full-time faculty were nontenured. At two-year colleges, part-time faculty appointments were more common than full-time non-tenure-track appointments. Thus, public two-year institutions had the lowest percentage overall, with 10.1 percent of their entire full-time faculty nontenured (Forrest Cataldi, Fahimi, and Bradburn, 2005).

We raise one point of interest regarding the increased representation of full-time non-tenure-track faculty. Even though full-time nontenure track has become the more common appointment for full-time new hires and the overall percentage of full-time nontenured faculty has increased among full-time faculty as a whole, the percentage of full-time non-tenure-track faculty among all faculty has not changed. If we were to look at the percentage of full-time non-tenure-track faculty compared with full-time tenured, full-time on-track, part-time and adjunct faculty, and graduate assistants, the overall percentage of all full-time faculty who are nontenure track remained fairly stable from 1997 to 2007. In an analysis of both National Center for Education Statistics (NCES) and IPEDS data, the AFT (American Federation of Teachers, 2009) found that the percentage of all full-time non-tenure-track appointments remained at a steady 14 to 15 percent over that span of ten years. At various institutional types, the percentage of full-time non-tenure-track faculty compared with all faculty may be slightly different, but their respective percentages also remained fairly constant. According to the AFT study (American

Federation of Teachers, 2009) of community colleges, full-time non-tenure-track faculty were 13 to 14 percent of total faculty. At public comprehensive institutions, full-time non-tenure-track faculty increased from 9 percent in 1997 to 11 percent in 2007. At public research institutions, the amount remained at 14 percent over ten years. Among private nonprofit institutions, the percentage of non-tenure-track full-time faculty remained at approximately 18 percent from 1997 to 2007 (American Federation of Teachers, 2009). Instead, the percentages of tenured and tenure-track faculty declined from 33.1 percent to 27.3 percent as part-time faculty rose from 34.1 percent to 36.9 percent and graduate assistants from 18.6 percent to 20.9 percent in those same years (American Federation of Teachers, 2009).

Academic fields. For full-time non-tenure-track faculty, various academic fields saw a greater increase in percentages than others. The greatest increase of non-tenure-track faculty was in the health sciences, beginning with 1.9 percent of all full-time faculty in 1969 to 22.4 percent of the full-time faculty in 1998 (Schuster and Finkelstein, 2006). In 1998 the second largest percentage was in the humanities, with full-time non-tenure-track faculty accounting for 15.9 percent of full-time faculty and the liberal arts and sciences for 11.8 percent (Schuster and Finkelstein, 2006).[3]

Shifting the perspective to focus more on each discipline as a distinct group, we can see the representation of full-time non-tenure-track faculty in their own programs. According to the NSOPF:04, full-time non-tenure-track faculty made up 44.1 percent of all the full-time faculty (faculty with tenure, those on the tenure track, those not on the tenure track, and those in institutions without a tenure system) in the health sciences in 2003 (Forrest Cataldi, Fahimi, and Bradburn, 2005). Non-tenure-track faculty in education made up 32.6 percent of the full-time faculty. For other program areas, full-time non-tenure-track faculty were 22.2 percent of the full-time faculty in the humanities, 16.2 percent in social sciences, 24.0 percent in natural sciences, 17.9 percent in fine arts, 15.4 percent in engineering, 22.5 percent in agriculture/home economics, and 17.3 percent in business (Forrest Cataldi, Fahimi, and Bradburn, 2005). In other programs not included in these subjects, non-tenure-track faculty accounted for 30.7 percent of all full-time faculty in those departments combined.

Unionized campuses. When talking about institutions, it is difficult to discuss campuses without addressing unions. As seen throughout this chapter and monograph, unions such as the AFT and the NEA have an interest in non-tenure-track faculty and in collecting data to better understand trends. Currently approximately a quarter of four-year higher education institutions have non-tenure-track faculty who are represented by unions (Hollenshead and others, 2007). Of that population, the highest were those schools considered Masters I and II (46 percent) and doctoral extensive (43 percent). Hollenshead and others (2007) note that unionized schools tend to hire a larger number of non-tenure-track faculty, even more so part-time faculty. Nonunion campuses tend to have almost equal amounts of part-time and full-time non-tenure-track faculty. They note, however, that those unionized non-tenure-track faculty are often paid more, given more benefits, and have better working conditions than their nonunionized counterparts. A study of union and faculty hiring (Dobbie and Robinson, 2008) found that the relationship between unions and reliance on non-tenure-track faculty had mixed results (see the chapter "Experiences of Non-Tenure-Track Faculty" for a more detailed discussion).

Overall, part-time and full-time non-tenure-track faculty combined are the new faculty majority in academia. As non-tenure-track appointments continue to be the majority of new hires, the proportion of non-tenure-track faculty to tenured and tenure-track faculty will continue to grow unless institutions make a concerted effort to change this trend.

Historical Developments

The increase in non-tenure-track faculty has occurred in two distinct waves. The first was the growth of part-time non-tenure-track faculty beginning with the community college sector of higher education. The second occurred in the 1990s when higher education saw an increase in full-time non-tenure-track faculty predominantly in four-year institutions. From these waves the proportion of non-tenure-track faculty (both full and part time) has grown significantly, while the proportion of tenured and tenure-track faculty has decreased (Schuster and Finkelstein, 2006; Outcalt, 2002; Ehrenberg, 2005).

Scholars have attributed this rise and fall to certain factors that have taken place and are still taking place in higher education. The first was the opening of higher education to the masses (Schell and Stock, 2001, Baldwin and Chronister, 2001), the second was the dwindling of existing resources (Cross and Goldenberg, 2009; Thedwall, 2008; Baldwin and Chronister, 2001; Gappa and Leslie, 1993), and the third was the corporatization of higher education (Baldwin and Chronister, 2001; Cross and Goldenberg, 2009; Slaughter and Rhoades, 2004). These three factors all contributed to the growth of both part-time and full-time non-tenure-track faculty. This section explores the various historical contexts that contributed to the growth of non-tenure-track faculty, first focusing on part-time developments in the community colleges (which take place in small, struggling private institutions as well) and then the growth of full-time non-tenure-track faculty predominantly in four-year institutions.

The Rise of Part-Time Faculty

The combination of unprecedented growth in student enrollments and the administrative miscalculation of that growth spurred the increase of non-tenure-track faculty hires (Cross and Goldenberg, 2009). Increased student enrollment in community colleges traces back to two major legislative works (Cohen and Brawer, 2008). First, the Servicemen's Readjustment Act of 1944 (the GI bill), issued after World War II, provided funding for educational opportunities (college or vocational training) for returning U.S. servicemen. Second, the 1947 President's Commission on Higher Education offered access to two additional years of education after the completion of high school. These acts began the democratization of higher education, and community colleges found themselves playing a large role in that process.

Community colleges became access points for those people who wanted further education but were unwilling or unable to pursue degrees at four-year institutions: vocational students, part-time students, women, ethnic and racial minorities, those of lower socioeconomic status, and those who performed poorly in high school (Cohen and Brawer, 2008; Brewster, 2000). Community colleges saw surges in enrollment, particularly in the 1960s and 1970s. This influx of students over the years stretched the capacity of the existing faculty. Institutions needed to find ways to accommodate the larger group of students by hiring more faculty, but in many ways community colleges were more limited in their options to accommodate these students compared with traditional four-year institutions (Cohen and Brawer, 2008; Levin, Kater, and Wagoner, 2006).

Because community colleges serve the population of students not served by traditional institutions, students often are economically disadvantaged. Although other institutions can raise tuition to meet the rising costs and decreased funding, community colleges have to maintain significantly lower tuitions than four-year institutions (Brewster, 2000; Christensen, 2008). Because of the predominantly vocational or transitional goals of community colleges as well as the teaching-dominant nature of faculty work and responsibilities, community colleges are also less likely to receive other funding in the form of research grants, alumni donations, and endowments to offset costs. Community colleges had two options to meet the demand, one of which "was considered painful to external stakeholders, and [the other] to internal stakeholders. The first was to raise the price of admission and the second was to cut costs" (Brewster, 2000, p. 67). Community colleges had to do the latter. Hiring part-time faculty instead of full-time tenure-track line faculty was one significant way to cut costs (Anderson, 2002; Gappa, 1984). In most cases, hiring part-time faculty costs significantly less than their full-time counterparts, because they receive lower wages and fewer benefits (Wyles, 1998; Monks, 2007). Part-time faculty are also cost-effective hires because a large nationwide search and a lengthy hiring process are often not needed (Gappa and Leslie, 1993; Hollenshead and others, 2007).

The influx of students also made it challenging for administrators to know the exact number of faculty needed for each semester. Community colleges needed to maintain flexibility in both their hiring practices and their schedule of classes (Levin, Kater, and Wagoner, 2006). Because of the nature of many part-time contracts, part-time faculty can often be hired or released on short notice, depending on enrollment for the semester, as "a way to 'staff up' for heavy fall enrollments and to 'slack off' for light spring loads" (McLaughlin, 2005, p. 186). Some people have criticized this hiring flexibility for creating a "faculty of convenience" of part-time hires, as staffing is determined by market demand (Wyles, 1998; Levin, Kater, and Wagoner, 2006). Because of the nontraditional student population at community colleges, the institutions also had to offer a variety of classes at a variety of times. With part-time faculty, community colleges are able to offer classes throughout the day and into the evening, with those less-desirable time slots filled by part-time faculty (Wallin, 2005).

All higher education institutions had to address similar factors: increased enrollments, limited resources, and the need for cutting costs and maintaining flexibility. So the proliferation of part-time faculty throughout all institutional types in the academy continued. In the 1990s, however, a new development was taking place—the rise of full-time non-tenure-track faculty in four-year institutions.

The Rise of Full-Time Faculty

Though echoing some of the elements of increases in part-time faculty in community colleges, the increase of full-time non-tenure-track faculty in proportion to full-time tenured or tenure-track faculty occurred more in the 1990s. With the recessions of the 1970s and 1980s, many administrators projected that enrollment would decrease during the recession, but they miscalculated enrollment numbers, which actually increased during times of recession (Thedwall, 2008; Cross and Goldenberg, 2009). Similar to the situation in community colleges, part of the increase in enrollment was also the result of the increase in nontraditional students entering four-year institutions (Baldwin and Chronister, 2001).

This surge also came at a time when many of the faculty hired in the 1960s and 1970s (including part-timers) were nearing the age of retirement. Estimates predicted that by 2000, half the tenured professoriate would be at least fifty-five years old but only 20 percent would retire that year (Baldwin and Chronister, 2001). Those tenured professors who did retire, with the help of some federal employment policies that encouraged early retirements, were not replaced with other tenure-track faculty. To meet this increase in enrollment and the uncertainty of an aging faculty that may or may not retire, administrators hired more full-time faculty with no promise of tenure (Thedwall, 2008). Because of a lack of tenure positions, the new faculty hired came from a large population of surplus Ph.D.s and other qualified candidates who were looking for some form of employment (Baldwin and Chronister, 2001).

The increase in student enrollments at a time when resources were limited is another reason for the rise in full-time non-tenure-track faculty, similar to the development of part-time faculty in community colleges. Baldwin and Chronister (2001) note that the reduction in government funding in the late 1980s to the 1990s was another reason institutions turned to full-time non-tenure-track faculty. Although institutions saw their funds reduced, the costs to maintain a college or university were increasing, and institutions had to meet those costs. Institutions raised tuition but still needed to limit expenses while still having instructors in the classrooms (Baldwin and Chronister, 2001). Hiring full-time non-tenure-track faculty was a way to meet those fiscal needs, and the buyer's market for faculty was an "enabling" factor as well (discussed later in this chapter).

The reduction in funding from federal and state governments helped influence colleges and universities to look to other operational models, more specifically a corporate business model. Colleges and universities had to find alternative ways to increase funding from sources other than government and tuition as well as to decrease costs. These sources included research grants and donations from alumni. Trustees pressured institutions to adopt business models and consider outsourcing employment and adopting new approaches to staffing (Slaughter and Rhoads, 2004). The new business model emphasized maximizing efficiency and valued those policies and programs that brought in revenue. The move toward a business model was further exacerbated by the increase of competition from for-profit higher education institutions with more financial flexibility, partially because of their non-tenure-track staff (Baldwin and Chronister, 2001).

Not only government funding lessened: in the 1980s and 1990s public support for higher education also lessened (Baldwin and Chronister, 2001). Baldwin and Chronister (2001) note that for the first time in many years, institutions faced a loss of public trust, a criticism of tenure, and challenges to faculty production and workload. With regard to public trust, the public began to question the commitment of higher education to undergraduate education (Bok, 1992, in Baldwin and Chronister, 2001). The public called into question rising tuition rates and seemingly large overhead income that exceeded the institution's needs. The public also perceived that faculty were more interested in research and obtaining grants than instructing undergraduates (Winston, 1992, in Baldwin and Chronister, 2001). This perception related to criticisms of tenure. Many people believed that tenure sheltered faculty too much from market and employment forces, allowing them to move away from undergraduate education toward their own pursuits. Institutions needed to hire faculty who were committed to undergraduate full-time instruction instead of research and who were not graduate students or part-time instructors. Linked with the first two elements that undermined public trust, discussions occurred about the nature of faculty productivity and workload. Critics wondered whether tenured faculty who did not teach undergraduates were an efficient use of limited funds. Policymakers and other stakeholders suggested that faculty be hired that are dedicated to instruction and for contracts to provide financial flexibility (Baldwin and Chronister, 2001).

Despite the historical factors (increases in student enrollments, an aging tenured faculty, decreased state and federal funding, increased competition, and the undermining of public trust), tensions of interpretation still exist regarding the historical development of the non-tenure-track faculty majority. Some researchers such as Slaughter and Rhoades (2004) and Benjamin (2002) argue that the rise in non-tenure-track faculty is a deliberate attempt to undermine tenure and a reflection of a new corporate model of higher education. Others such as Cross and Goldenberg (2009) argue that the non-tenure-track majority was the unintended consequence of various factors and events that happened to intersect. The truth may be somewhere in the space that lies between.

In the past few years, colleges and universities have been moving toward a different model of education similar to businesses, seen in examples of "branding" and a push for research to be funded by outside resources (Slaughter and Rhoades, 2004). In many ways, people then make hiring decisions based on the current model of the institution. Likewise, numerous external factors have caused the academy to be more reactive than proactive such as weakening public trust and economic recessions (Baldwin and Chronister, 2001; Cross and Goldenberg, 2009). Armed with a corporate-like model and imperfect information, administrators may have made decisions geared toward shaping the faculty composition in a particular way but were probably not aware of the magnitude of effect such decisions would have when made over a period of years. Cross and Goldenberg (2009) argue that miscalculations and failures to incorporate the numbers of both the enrollment and faculty into the university infrastructure the following years also led to the increase in non-tenure-track faculty.

The Demand for Non-Tenure-Track Faculty

These non-tenure-track faculty appointments would not be so prolific if there were not some benefits and reasons for actually creating more of the faculty appointments. Earlier in this chapter we discussed the historical events that encouraged institutions to find alternatives to tenure positions; this section explores the reasons for explicitly hiring non-tenure-track faculty—some explicitly economic and some not.

Most, if not all, scholars agree that economic reasons play a very large role in the hiring of non-tenure-track faculty (Gappa and Leslie, 1993; Baldwin and Chronister, 2001; Cross and Goldenberg, 2002, 2009; Hollenshead and others, 2007; Benjamin, 2002; Burgan, 2006; Slaughter and Rhoades, 2004). The first economic reason is connected to cost-effectiveness. For the price of one tenure-track faculty member, the university could afford more non-tenure-track faculty who would be able to instruct more classes, thus meeting the demands of increasing enrollment (Cross and Goldenberg, 2009; Pratt, 1997). For full-time non-tenure-track faculty among the eighty-six four-year college and universities surveyed, approximately 70 percent of the baccalaureate and master's institutions paid salaries comparable to tenure-eligible faculty, while only 36 percent of doctoral institutions and 44 percent of research institutions were comparable (Baldwin and Chronister, 2001). At the doctoral and research level, a majority of the schools surveyed had lower salaries for their full-time non-tenure-track faculty.

For part-time faculty the difference is even greater: the national average for the basic salary of part-time faculty is $11,200, while the national average basic salary of a full-time faculty member (tenure and nontenure track) is $67,400 (Forrest Cataldi, Fahimi, and Bradburn, 2005). The lack of benefits is another way hiring non-tenure-track faculty can be cost-effective for the institution;

very few part-time faculty receive benefits through the institution (Gappa and Leslie, 1993; Hollenshead and others, 2007, Monks, 2007). A large majority of, though not all, institutions, however, provide benefits for full-time non-tenure-track faculty. Non-tenure-track faculty are also cost-effective in terms of the hiring process, as a large nationwide search with a lengthy hiring process is often not needed for part-time faculty appointments, though many institutions are beginning to conduct large nationwide searches for full-time non-tenure-track faculty (Gappa and Leslie, 1993; Hollenshead and others, 2007).

The second economic reason is flexibility. Depending on student enrollment, demand for a class, and unexpected changes in the budget for that semester or year, departments are able to add and remove instructors to remain in the allotted budget (Hollenshead and others, 2007; Gappa and Leslie, 1993; Tolbert, 1998; Baldwin, 1998). Departments are able to more readily respond to any changes and fluctuations in the market with non-tenure-track faculty. Because many full-time faculty are not on multiyear contracts, schools are able to have yearly flexibility, while part-time faculty, whose employment typically depends on academic terms (semesters, trimesters, quarters, for example), provide even more flexibility.

Many reasons, not directly tied to fiscal issues, exist for institutions to hire non-tenure-track faculty as well. Despite feelings of second-class citizenship that some non-tenure-track faculty experience on certain campuses, researchers found that many administrators have very favorable impressions of both full-time and part-time non-tenure-track faculty (Cross and Goldenberg, 2009; Hollenshead and others, 2007). In Hollenshead and others' study (2007), 80 percent of the administrators interviewed had positive opinions. The themes focused on teaching ability and professional expertise in a particular field. With specific examples such as renowned musicians or politicians, the school gains prestige from having such part-time faculty. The institutions themselves use non-tenure-track positions to meet the needs of dual-academic-career couples, when the chances of both partners' obtaining a tenure-track position at the same institution are little to none (Wolf-Wendel, Twombly, and Rice, 2003). Hollenshead and others (2007) further corroborated Gappa and Leslie's finding (1993) that hiring non-tenure-track faculty allowed for the tenured faculty to be free to pursue research interests. Hollenshead and others (2007) also note that hiring non-tenure-track faculty benefits the institution by strengthening connections to the community, as faculty (mainly part-time faculty) come from local areas. Schools also benefit from information about other institutions like hospitals or nonprofit organizations, as faculty hires usually come from other organizations that can enrich higher education institutions. Finally, non-tenure-track faculty can be a way for institutions to test out newer fields and departments, to determine success without investing as much revenue in tenured faculty.

Both Cross and Goldenberg (2009) and Gappa and Leslie (1993) note that an element of unintentionality is present: administrations establish hiring practices in times of what they believed to be temporary financial stress, unknowingly shifting the number of faculty positions toward non-tenure-track and decentralized hiring practices.

Typologies and Titles of Non-Tenure-Track Faculty

We mentioned earlier that part of the challenge in understanding non-tenure-track faculty is the lack of common and acceptable terms to use when discussing the growing majority of faculty. Those faculty who are not on the tenure track are a heterogeneous mixture of individuals with varying experiences (differences explored in the next chapter, "Experiences of Non-Tenure-Track Faculty"), and it is that heterogeneity that can make conceptualizing the faculty a challenge. In the literature, researchers usually identify the various types of non-tenure-track faculty in two particular ways: by functional typologies that reflect individual motivation or context or by job titles given by the employment terms of the specific institution or higher education system. Sometimes typologies and titles can overlap; the title "instructor," for example, can be a typology based on primary faculty responsibility and at the same time the title the institution gives to part-time non-tenure-track faculty.

Functional Typologies

Some researchers took an inductive approach to understanding different groups of non-tenure-track faculty and created functional typologies to better classify and understand different sectors. They created their own typologies based on their empirical data, looking at different aspects for categorization such as responsibility, motivation, circumstance, or experience (Tuckman, 1978; Gappa and Leslie, 1993; Levin, Kater, and Wagoner, 2006; Baldwin and Chronister, 2001). Typologies are important because they allow us to better categorize and classify phenomena in our experience. Good typologies are meaningful in nature; they can add clarity and organization to our conceptualizations. Applying a typology to studies of non-tenure-track faculty based on these elements gives further insight into some of the motivations and circumstances of the faculty and may also give insight into the difficulties involved with unilateral plans of actions or solutions toward incorporating them better into the institution. Researchers based these typologies predominantly on the responsibilities, motivations, and experiences of the faculty (Tuckman, 1978; Gappa and Leslie, 1993; Baldwin and Chronister, 2001).

One of the first typologies was created in Tuckman's study (1978) of part-time faculty; he found seven primary categories of part-time faculty: semiretireds, graduate students, hopeful full-timers, full mooners, homeworkers, part mooners, and part unknowners (for a more in-depth explanation, see Tuckman [1978] or Gappa and Leslie [1993]). In a later study of part-time faculty, Gappa and Leslie (1993) found that the individual experiences and patterns of the faculty were too complex to encapsulate in the narrower categories Tuckman offered, so they proposed their own, subsuming Tuckman's typology into four broad categories: career enders; specialists, experts, and professionals; aspiring academics; and freelancers.

According to Gappa and Leslie (1993), *career enders* include individuals in the process of retiring as well as retirees. Many of them come from established careers outside academia and have decided to continue in academia for a combination of reasons: the supplemental income, keeping a hand in the field, or simply because they enjoy the experience. *Specialists, experts, and professionals* are employed full-time elsewhere and come from a varied range of careers. They are hired for their specialized knowledge or success in certain fields, whether the arts or business. Rather than relying on the faculty position for income, these faculty often take the position simply because they enjoy teaching. Some of these specialists can also add prestige to the institution. These faculty may be well known in their fields, and the institution benefits by having the person on its faculty roster. The University of Southern California School of Cinematic Arts, for example, has a cadre of award-winning faculty involved in the entertainment industry, many of them part-time non-tenure-track faculty. *Aspiring academics* include faculty who are looking for a full-time or tenure-track position such as graduate students and individuals looking for a position at the same school as their partners. Faculty who manage to create full-time schedules from part-time faculty positions—"freeway fliers"—are also included in this category (Gappa and Leslie, 1993). Finally, *freelancers,* predominantly faculty who supplement the part-time positions with other jobs not in academia or who may be caretakers at home, use the position for supplemental income.

Baldwin and Chronister (2001) established a typology to better understand full-time non-tenure-track faculty based on the terms of employment responsibilities: teachers, researchers, administrators, and other academic professionals. *Teachers* spend more than two-thirds of their time in instruction and the rest of their time split between administrative tasks and research. *Researchers* are specifically hired to conduct research for over half their time, with the other half divided between instruction and administration. *Administrators* spend about half their time in administrative works (often being on committees) and spend the rest of the time in research and other activities. *Other academic professionals*—full-time non-tenure-track faculty who spend half their time with activities other than teaching, research, or administration—could be lab technicians, programmers, or community service members. They usually spend a quarter of their time teaching, depending on their qualifications (Baldwin and Chronister, 2001).

Another way to categorize faculty is in terms of voluntary and involuntary non-tenure-track employment (either full-time or part-time) (Tilly, 1998; Maynard and Joseph, 2008). Though tenure has been a traditional goal for those in academe since it was first introduced (Burgan, 2006; Chait, 2005; Benjamin, 2003b), some faculty actively choose not to take a full-time position or tenure-track position (Gappa, Austin, and Trice, 2007; Chait and Trower; 1997; Bataille and Brown, 2006; Hollenshead and others, 2007). These faculty would be considered voluntary non-tenure-track employees.

Conley and Leslie (2002) note that some part-time faculty simply enjoy teaching and do not depend on the position as a career, while others choose to be part time because it best fits into their lives or is only a supplementary career. Levin, Kater, and Wagoner (2006) divided part-time non-tenure-track faculty in community colleges into those who had careers in other professions and those who relied on the part-time position for their sole income. Hollenshead and others (2007) found that faculty also chose to be nontenured to seek a balance between work and life or to adapt to geographic constraints. Chait and Trower (1997) found that for those faculty in institutions that offered them the option between tenure and non-tenure tracks, they chose the latter for other benefits such as a "10 percent salary supplement, summer stipend, and the one year's severance pay [if a long-term contract was not renewed]" (p. 16), while others wanted to either teach more or to have an overall lessened load. Gappa, Austin, and Trice (2007) found that at some institutions, depending on department and campus context, full-time non-tenure-track faculty did not have as many challenges as part-time faculty or some of the disadvantages of the tenure track. These individuals opted for full-time non-tenure-track status and perceived full-time non-tenure-track positions most preferable.

Involuntary non-tenure-track employees also exist. If they are full time or part time, they may be faculty who are looking for tenured positions in their field and currently hold the appointment waiting for a tenure-track opening (Gappa, Austin, and Trice, 2007; Gappa and Leslie, 1993; Conley and Leslie, 2002). Gappa and Leslie's group of "aspiring academics" could be considered in this classification. As illustrated in Tuckman's and Gappa and Leslie's typologies (1978 and 1993, respectively), some faculty prefer a tenure-track position but are unable to find one for various reasons, many of them closely tied to the historical developments covered at the beginning of this chapter. The biggest factor seems to be that the percentage of tenure-track and tenured positions has decreased in the past years. Hollenshead and others (2007) noted that "by 2003, full- and part-time non-tenure-track appointments accounted for three out of five (65 percent) faculty positions in all types of institutions" (p. 4; see also American Association of University Professors, 2006). So at that time, many academics who initially entered the field wanting a tenured position faced dwindling job possibilities. Moreover, in terms of part-time faculty's being involuntarily nontenure track, some part-time faculty prefer full-time non-tenure-track employment (Conley and Leslie, 2002). The perceptions and experiences between voluntary and involuntary non-tenure-track faculty may vary greatly.

The question still remains, however: With the difficulties many experience, why stay? Many non-tenure-track faculty enjoy teaching and working with students in the higher education environment (Gappa, Austin, and Trice, 2007; Gappa and Leslie, 1993). Other faculty, for various reasons, lack the necessary requirements such as degrees or credentials, or had not kept up with research that would avail them of full-time or tenure-track appointments (Gappa and Leslie, 1993). Still other faculty may be nontenure track because their partner is on the tenure track at the same campus or at a campus nearby (Wolf-Wendel, Twombly, and Rice, 2003).

Titles

The titles full-time and part-time faculty are not uniform across all campuses and even, at times, on the same campus. Depending on the institution or institutional system, titles assigned to non-tenure-track faculty may vary significantly. For example, a "lecturer" at one campus may indicate part-time faculty, while another campus may use the term "instructor." In a single campus, the definition of "clinical faculty" may be different depending on department or school. Berry (2005) lists fifty titles and terms given to part-time faculty alone, with examples such as "casual," "sessional," or "adjunct" professors (for a complete list of full-time tenure-track and part-time faculty, see Berry, 2005, p. xi). Not only do titles vary from campus to campus; similar titles may signify different positions depending on the higher education system. For example, the term "fixed term" or "adjunct" may indicate a full-time non-tenure-track faculty member on one campus and a part-time faculty member on another campus (Shavers, 2000). The decentralized nature of hiring leads to the proliferation of titles as various disciplines have developed different conventions.

Specific titles are often linked to the employment stipulations or contract language of a particular campus or system. For example, some higher education systems such as New Hampshire distinguish between tenure-track and non-tenure-track faculty as "status appointments" and "nonstatus appointments," respectively, in their human resource documents. Institutions often define and establish such titles for themselves, which may explain why so many different terms exist. They can be found in contract language or campus-related media (such as Web pages, employment postings, and contact lists). Inconsistent use of titles across higher education is only one of the challenges when trying to understand non-tenure-track faculty.

Although academic titles may be used idiosyncratically at many institutions, how those titles are used matters. Academic titles, to be helpful, should be precise; they should reflect a classification based on type or category. These titles are rarely examined for accuracy, consistency, and applicability, however. For tenure-track faculty, titles are often clear and consistent across a majority of institutions. For example, Shavers (2000) found that the titles of tenure-track faculty—"assistant," "associate," and "full" professor—reflected a particular meaning and were consistently and typically used across all the tenure-granting institutions and Carnegie classifications. The titles indicate experience, research, publications, presentations, contribution to the field, and service to the school and scholarly community. The assignment of tenure-track titles is in stark contrast to many of the titles for non-tenure-track faculty, especially part-time non-tenure-track faculty, many of which make no distinction for promotion or seniority, job focus, or contract terms. It assumes that it is not necessary to differentiate among non-tenure-track faculty.[4]

For full-time non-tenure-track faculty, Shavers (2000) found that though policy language is often "nebulous" regarding qualifications, roles, and reappointment, some distinctions exist in rank and titles, especially for those full-time-non-tenure track faculty in professional fields. As a matter of fact, research and clinical faculty often follow the same ladder system as tenure-track faculty, with "research" or "clinical" being a modifier. Fifteen of 196 institutions sampled from the Faculty Appointment Policy Archive used titles associated with tenure-track faculty. The more common terms used for full-time non-tenured faculty, however, are "lecturer" or "instructor" (Shavers, 2000).

Other employment classifications inform titles such as tenure or full-time equivalent (FTE) hours. One of the broadest distinctions is between tenure-track or tenured faculty and non-tenure-track faculty, because it delineates different job security and career paths. Using the distinction between tenure-track and non-tenure-track faculty, however, would not work well on campuses where tenure is not applicable. In those institutions that have only full-time or part-time non-tenure-track faculty such as for-profit institutions and 9 percent of private colleges (Chait and Trower, 1997), distinguishing between tenure and nontenure does not apply. Nonprofit institutions without tenure may also have faculty structures that are qualitatively different from the other institutions; including them as simply non-tenure-track faculty ignores contextual differences.

Another broad distinction separating the faculty is between full-time (at times with tenure and nontenure combined) and part-time faculty, with the distinction depending on various factors such as percentage of FTEs or number of courses or credit hours taught (Hollenshead and others, 2007). As Hollenshead and others (2007) note, however, schools often used multiple markers (such as number of courses or contract length) to determine status, and each school uses a different formula. Even the distinction between full-time and part-time using FTEs varies depending on the laws of a particular state or rules of an institution. For example, in California community colleges, part-time instructors are not to work more than 66 percent of a full-time load, while at University of Ohio, the limit is 75 percent. This difference often leads to "part time" being a misnomer. Full-time faculty must work at 100 percent, including participation in activities outside of the classroom where they often receive compensation; but some part-timers work up to 80 or 90 percent, often participating in faculty activities where they are uncompensated. Meanwhile, many other fields consider anything over 75 percent full time.

Titles may also reflect work responsibilities that the university expects of the faculty. Some titles reflect teaching, such as lecturer or instructor. These positions focus mainly on student instruction, with little expectation of research or publications. Other titles reflect research-specific faculty or practitioners such as research faculty, clinical faculty, and specialist. Rather than instruction, the focus of these faculty is on research, conducting studies, working at centers or in laboratories, and producing publications or products. Practitioners like artists and musicians producing works are labeled "professor of practice," while in the field of medicine, faculty are practicing professionals or professor of clinical studies. Students who are teachers or researchers are called "teaching assistants," "research assistants," or "graduate assistants."

Researchers of non-tenure-track faculty often use these academic titles in their work to differentiate among different groups of faculty, but few acknowledge the typologies that have been established by researchers such as Gappa and Leslie, and Baldwin and Chronister. Functional typologies of responsibilities and expectations can be useful when trying to understand non-tenure-track faculty in terms of research or establishing expectations. When conducting research to measure productivity or quality of non-tenure-track faculty, it is important to ensure that the samples are either homogeneous or comparable with respect to function or activity to get a more valid result. For example, results would be significantly different among studies measuring the publication amounts if the samples consisted of teaching faculty, research faculty, or combination of both. We should also use these typologies carefully, with the understanding that the titles do not encompass the entirety of expectations and responsibilities and that there actually may be both overlap or requirements that go beyond the limitations of the title. For example, clinical professors may also teach or be directors of research centers or serve the campus in an administrative capacity.

Likewise, institutions should establish consistent policies regarding titles assigned to non-tenure-track faculty. First, consistent and structured academic titles would allow for institutions to ensure more reliable data collection on the current faculty composition of the campus. One of the challenges regarding the study of non-tenure-track faculty is the fact that often institutions themselves do not have a reliable way to obtain accurate data as a result of differing academic titles. Second, established titles with a consistent system indicating seniority or other distinctions in position would ease the application of any seniority or promotional system a campus may want to implement. Finally, carefully planned titles acknowledge the distinctions among non-tenure-track faculty and their work rather than melding them together under an umbrella term.

The varied typology of non-tenure-track faculty is key to understanding the other chapters in this monograph: the different experiences and the various plans of action regarding non-tenure-track faculty. It is also one of the key challenges of researching non-tenure-track faculty. The numerous particulars of erminology alone make it difficult for researchers to collect nationwide data or or schools to report consistent data on the status of non-tenure-track faculty. It also places an onus on researchers to be careful when obtaining a sample population to ensure that the non-tenure-track faculty they are researching are comparable to each other. In addition, the varied motivations and experiences are a challenge to any universal plan of action for institutions.

Data and Trends Related to Non-Tenure-Track Faculty

It is readily agreed that the overall percentage of non-tenure-track faculty has been rising over the past few years. It is also important to begin to break down that percentage to note any particular changes in the group and any larger trends occurring with the faculty as a whole. This section first looks specifically at the composition (for example, race and gender) of non-tenure-track faculty. Second, it focuses on career mobility of these faculty, from part-time to full-time and from nontenure to tenure track. Third, it looks at faculty degrees, data that are often a basis for many of the arguments for and against the use of non-tenure-track faculty in higher education.

Faculty Composition

Over the past twenty years, higher education has seen more women and ethnic minorities receive graduate degrees than in previous years. With this increase in individuals holding advanced degrees, it would make sense that we would see a larger percentage of women and minorities in faculty positions. Likewise, with the increase of graduate degrees conferred, one may see a trend regarding the age of faculty in specific academic appointments. Understanding these factors and their relation to the type of faculty appointments may prove to be important in discussing possible trends that take place.

Women. Women continue to be disproportionately represented in non-tenure-track faculty appointments, both full time and part time. In 1996–1997, 40.8 percent of those graduating with a doctoral degree were women; in 2006–2007, that percentage increased to 50.1 percent (National Center for

Education Statistics, 2009). With regard to overall non-tenure-track positions, however, Schuster and Finkelstein (2006) noted that women were twice as likely as men to be on the off-tenure track. In the *Non-Tenure-Track Faculty Report* (Association of American Universities, 2001), which looked at a sample of thirty AAU research universities, 45 percent of all non-tenure-track faculty were women. In their 1993 study of part-time faculty, Gappa and Leslie found that women, though they did not account for a majority of part-time faculty, their numbers were disproportionally represented compared with the total number of women in the academy. They also found that women were concentrated as part-time faculty at liberal arts colleges and public doctoral institutions. Years later, the trends continue. According to Forrest, Cataldi, Fahimi, and Bradburn (2005), part-time faculty comprised 48 percent women and 52 percent men in fall 2003.

Similar results can be seen in full-time non-tenure-track appointments. Harper, Baldwin, Gansneder, and Chronister (2001) note that the number and proportion of women in non-tenure-track positions grew disproportionately. Their study found that women were slightly younger than men in the same position and that in cases of faculty ranks for non-tenure-track faculty women were least likely to move to the highest available position. The same trends can be seen in the AAUP's *Annual Report on the Economic Status of the Profession, 2004–2005* (2005). In terms of racial and ethnic differences, minority women were less likely to be full-time non-tenure-track faculty than minority men, with the exception of Native American faculty (but a caveat is necessary because of the small percentage).

Scholars have proposed various factors to explain the large presence of women in non-tenure-track appointments, which relates closely to the topic of tenure. In a study of faculty, the AAUP found that women were still 10 to 15 percent less likely to be in tenure-eligible positions than men (American Association of University Professors, 2005). Gappa, Austin, and Trice (2007) noted that often obtaining tenure can be more difficult for women than for men. Until recently, many women felt they had to choose between raising family and obtaining tenure because both require large amounts of time (Harper, Baldwin, Gansneder, and Chronister, 2001; Ehrenberg, 2005). Another reason for the high proportion of women in non-tenure-track positions is that women tend to be in fields that have more non-tenure-track faculty such as composition, the humanities, and health sciences (National Center for Education Statistics, 2009). Even with family policies such as maternity leave, women tend to be at a disadvantage in the pursuit of tenure or choose a non-tenure-track position instead.

Racial and ethnic differences. Given the substantial increase of racial and ethnic minorities graduating with advanced degrees, the overall faculty composition has yet to completely reflect the diversity found in graduation rates, especially in tenure-track positions (Gappa, Austin, and Trice, 2007). In 1996–1997, 38.7 percent of those graduating with a doctoral degree were racial or ethnic minorities; in 2006–2007, that percentage increased to 44.8 percent (National Center for Education Statistics, 2009). Many of the researchers found the disparity between gender in non-tenure-track and tenure-track appointments to be a greater cause for concern than issues of race and ethnicity (Baldwin and Chronister, 2001; Schuster and Finkelstein, 2006; American Federation of Teachers, 2003).

Despite the point regarding minority women in full-time non-tenure-track positions, the overall trend leans slightly toward racial and ethnic minorities being overrepresented in non-tenure-track faculty positions. With regard to part-time faculty, the numbers seem to be similar to the full-time non-tenure-track sector. Gappa and Leslie (1993) found that only 9.2 percent of part-time faculty were ethnic or racial minorities and raised concerns at the seeming lack of diversity that was happening in part-time appointments. The 2009 AFT study found that among the part-time hires, African American faculty increased by 0.5 percent; Asian–Pacific Islander by 0.2 percent, Hispanic by 0.4 percent, and Native American by even less. Interestingly, researchers have found that the group labeled "nonresident aliens" grew in number from 1997 to 2007, from 8 percent to 14 percent (American Federation of Teachers, 2009) attributing the increase to hires in part-time faculty (1.3 percent) and graduate assistants (2.3 percent). In 2007, the percentage of ethnic minorities among part-time faculty was still at 9 percent (American Federation of Teachers, 2009).

Of full-time non-tenure-track faculty, Asian faculty were 7.3 percent, other nonWhite faculty were 9.8 percent, and White faculty were 82.9 percent

(Schuster and Finkelstein, 2006). Baldwin and Chronister (2001) noted that faculty of color in full-time non-tenure-track appointments increased by 87 percent but only 40 percent in tenure-track positions. White faculty increased 36 percent in full-time non-tenure-track positions and 4 percent in tenure-track positions. In the time between 1992 and 1998, Native Americans/Alaska Natives, Whites, and Hispanics increased in non-tenure-track positions. Meanwhile, African Americans and Asian–Pacific Islanders decreased in non-tenure-track positions.

An interesting inference could be made from all the data of both full-time and part-time faculty. If taken as one population, that is, combining the number of full-time and part-time faculty, the faculty seem to be on their way to something resembling a diverse workforce. Once the numbers are separated and compared with one another, however, we find it is not necessarily true when it comes to part-time faculty. One reason for this disparity in numbers is that institutions focus on including racial and ethnic minorities in full-time and tenure-track positions but are less aware of the diversity in part-time faculty.

Career Mobility for Non-Tenure-Track Faculty

As noted previously, some non-tenure-track faculty are looking for full-time employment if they are part-time or tenure-track employment if they are non-tenure track (both full time and part time). Those "aspiring academics" or "involuntary" non-tenure-track faculty are the ones hoping to eventually move into a more secure faculty position. Using data about faculty in 1998,[5] Schuster and Finkelstein (2006) found that among current part-time faculty, approximately 60 percent of doctorate holders and 83 percent of master's degree holders reported having part-time employment as their only type of appointment in academia. Even when controlling for first-time appointments, only 34.9 percent of those part-time faculty with prior appointments had previous full-time academic appointments.[6] These numbers indicate an "'exclusive' pattern of part-time employment for part-time faculty" (Schuster and Finkelstein, 2006, p. 208).

Full-time faculty (which in Schuster and Finkelstein's calculation includes tenure, tenure-track, and nontenured faculty) also showed a pattern of full-time employment, with approximately 84 percent of doctorate holders and 78 percent of master's degree holders having full-time employment as their only type of appointment in academia. Among those full-time faculty who had previous academic experience, only 10.6 percent of those holding doctorates and 22.1 percent of those holding a master's degree reported previous part-time experience (Schuster and Finkelstein, 2006).

With regard to moving on and off the tenure track, the results are a little more complicated. Overall, Schuster and Finkelstein found that better permeability existed between non-tenure- to tenure-track appointments compared with part-time to full-time appointments. Of all faculty, 33.3 percent moved from off to on the tenure track; however, some factors may affect permeability. Institutional type determined mobility, with 76 percent of the entire faculty moving from nontenure to tenure-track positions in four-year institutions. With regard to program of study, the liberal arts and sciences accounted for 64 percent of those moving tracks. Individual factors also play a role. First, men are more likely to move from tenured to nontenured status than women (64 percent of those who moved were men). Second, permeability is also determined by traditional academic productivity (publications, research, grants, and so on). Third, those with doctoral degrees were more likely to move from one track to the other, as 76 percent of those who moved had a doctoral or professional degree. The importance of degrees in mobility may also play a part in the number and types of degrees held by non-tenure-track faculty.

Faculty Degrees and Academic Backgrounds

One key argument raised against the use of non-tenure-track faculty in higher education focuses on the academic credentials of non-tenure-track faculty. Scholars such as Benjamin (2002) argue that non-tenure-track faculty lack the necessary academic qualifications to serve students well. Further exploration of that claim is covered in Kezar and Sam (2010b), but this section specifically looks at the academic qualifications of both part-time and full-time faculty. This section first looks at the actual non-tenure-track faculty population and their qualifications and then looks at institutions' expectations or requirements to hold the faculty appointment.

Degrees of non-tenure-track faculty. According to a report by the AFT (American Federation of Teachers, 2003), full-time non-tenure-track faculty did not obtain the same degrees overall as tenure-track faculty from the stand-point of education level achieved. Based on data from 1992 to 1998, the AFT (American Federation of Teachers, 2003) found that on average 41 percent of the full-time non-tenure-track faculty had a doctorate or first professional degree, compared with 71 percent of tenure-track faculty. Baldwin and Chronister's findings (2001) reflect this information, though they note that only 33 percent had their doctorate, while 60 percent held either a master's degree or professional equivalent.

Though the full-time percentages did not match those on the tenure track, a higher percentage of full-time non-tenure-track faculty have their doctorate or first professional degree than part-time faculty. Gappa and Leslie (1993) found that 28.5 percent of part-time faculty held doctorates or professional degrees and that 42.7 percent had a master's. Using data from the NSOPF:99 on faculty whose "principal responsibility is instruction," Benjamin (2003b, p. 82) found that percentage to be much higher, with 47.1 percent holding a doctorate or first professional degree and 43.6 percent a master's only. This percentage is still lower than the 82.5 percent of full-time faculty, however based on his calculations. The expectations of both full-time and part-time faculty actually may explain the difference between the two.

Hiring expectations for non-tenure-track faculty. Hollenshead and others (2007) note that academic qualifications and employment requirements differ distinctly between part-time and full-time faculty. They found that hiring standards appear more rigorous for full-time non-tenure-track faculty than for part-time faculty. For example, they found that one in four administrators required a terminal degree for full-time non-tenure-track faculty but that, for part-time hires, only one in ten administrators required a terminal degree.

The actual faculty searches themselves also appear more rigorous for full-time faculty than for part-time faculty, though not as labor intensive as for tenure-track faculty (Hollenshead and others, 2007; Benjamin, 2002). Hollenshead and others (2007) found that more than 50 percent of the administrators in the study conducted formal nationwide searches, similar to tenure-track faculty searches. On a separate question, 75 percent of administrators held more local, yet still formal, searches. Administrators were also more likely to ask for references for full-time positions. This practice is in contrast with part-time faculty searches, where administrators often turned to people that they already know (Hollenshead and others, 2007).

Such disparities between required qualifications and faculty appointments play a role in explaining the salary disparity among the groups of faculty. They also could play a part in the segmented culture that many non-tenure-track faculty experience.

Conclusion

When we bring together various facets of the non-tenure-track faculty, an interesting phenomenon occurs. Just as a better picture is being created, nuances seem also to be brought into the foreground. An important key to both this chapter and the rest of this monograph (including Kezar and Sam, 2010b) is the various typologies and titles discussed. Much like a lens, the way we view non-tenure-track faculty changes when we alter our focus. To look at non-tenure-track faculty as nontenure track versus tenure track is to emphasize the issue of tenure when appropriate. To see faculty in terms of full time and part time highlights the distinctions of effort and workload, with their different experiences and demographics. We are also able to see the similarities and differences of faculty in terms of gender, race, and ethnicity. As we understand certain differences, for example, degrees, academic backgrounds, and credentials, we can identify different opportunities (such as institutional appointments or promotion) for certain non-tenure-track faculty. If we look at different motivations such as the "career ender" and the "aspiring academic," we can imagine a different interaction with the institution and colleagues. Likewise, the motivational lens highlights interplay between part-time faculty and tenured faculty, which was otherwise obscured when we combined full- and part-time non-tenure-track faculty. When we see the faculty in terms of context and motivation, we can begin to understand the reasons that some people choose to be on the nontenure track and still others wish for another employment option. As we continue, these lenses will frame our understanding of the various issues of non-tenure-track faculty: their experiences and different plans of action proposed later in this monograph.

Experiences of Non-Tenure-Track Faculty

It is difficult for some to understand that "different" doesn't mean "less than." In order to do so, what we'll need most of all is a mutual respect among all the members of the department, and that, in a culture based on traditional academic values, is perhaps the hardest thing to achieve.

—Maid, 2001, p. 88

GAPPA AND LESLIE (1993) NAMED THEIR BOOK *The Invisible Faculty* to capture the experience of part-time faculty at colleges and universities. Part-timers felt they were unacknowledged by colleagues. As a result of their research, Gappa and Leslie judged the bifurcated system as untenable, as part-time faculty are the have-nots with low pay, no job security, heavy workloads, and low status. They expressed concern that not only administrators but also tenure-track faculty supported this bifurcated system in which tenure-track faculty essentially ignored or demonized part-time faculty as lower quality. They documented a largely negative experience for part-time faculty, which we examine in this chapter.

This chapter describes research about the experience, working conditions, and role of non-tenure-track faculty to make them more visible to policymakers, members of the academy, and laypeople. Although non-tenure-track faculty are often ignored, an understanding of research on their experience can contribute to better institutional policymaking. It is important to note that much of the data on experience are gathered through qualitative research, with relatively small samples garnered through case studies. Only a handful of national quantitative studies have been conducted that examine non-tenure-track faculty experience (American Federation of Teachers, 2010; Hollenshead and others, 2007; Conley and Leslie, 2002). Most research identifies working conditions and infers experiences rather than the researchers talking directly to non-tenure-track faculty. Surprisingly, little systematic research has been conducted of non-tenure-track faculty themselves. We review the extant literature on the experiences of non-tenure-track faculty, being sensitive to variation by full- and part-time status, institutional type, and department or discipline. Institutional type and discipline have typically been overlooked; much more research reports on differences between full- and part-time faculty (Hollenshead and others, 2007; Benjamin, 2003a, 2003b; Clarke and Gabert, 2004).

A variety of studies have identified that working conditions, roles, and experiences of non-tenure-track faculty tend to be better on campuses that have unions and collective bargaining (Gappa and Leslie, 1993; Hollenshead and others, 2007). This trend does not necessarily mean that faculty on these campuses are more satisfied but that their salaries or benefits tend to be higher on campuses with collective bargaining. Additionally, processes such as role definition and recruitment and hiring are generally more intentional and thoughtful on campuses with collective bargaining.

In addition to collective bargaining making a major difference in the working conditions of non-tenure-track faculty, the *type* of contract affects the experience. Part-time faculty experience less access to benefits and even worse working conditions. Throughout, the chapter emphasizes differences between part-time and full-time non-tenure-track faculty (when they are specified in the research), as they are a major source of variation in the experiences of non-tenure-track faculty. And it is one area of difference that has been studied in greater depth by a few researchers.

The *discipline* and individual *motivation* also shape experience. Faculty in liberal arts fields such as composition or math have more negative departmental cultures than professional fields such as law or education, where non-tenure-track faculty are often given more respect and better working conditions. The motivation behind taking a non-tenure-track role influences the experience of faculty, particularly their satisfaction, but we know less about the impact of motivation because of limited research that looks at differences in the non-tenure-track group. *Institutional type* and *culture* also appear to shape experience. For example, institutions that are in more isolated places have to create a more intentional process for hiring and socializing non-tenure-track faculty, making the experience of non-tenure-track faculty more positive. Additionally, research universities pay full-time non-tenure-track faculty less than bachelor's and master's institutions. It is hard to make any generalizations about contract type, as discipline, motivation, institutional type, and union status all alter experiences and working conditions. Many of the differences (such as age, background, and academic credentials) have not even been investigated, so we report only those that have been explored to date.

The chapter is organized into three parts: working conditions, perspectives on faculty life, and concerns and unmet needs. The first section examines the main areas that are part of a faculty member's experience and working conditions—hiring, orientation, salary and benefits, governance, professional development, office space, and equipment. The next section covers research that specifically identifies how non-tenure-track faculty experience these working conditions and the general campus climate. Last, the chapter reviews studies that explore what non-tenure-track faculty themselves say are areas of concern that they hope will be addressed in the future.

Working Conditions

Working conditions like salary, support services, and professional development all affect the experience of non-tenure-track faculty. The most research has been conducted in this area in an effort to document the various facets that make up the experiences of non-tenure-track faculty.

Recruitment, Hiring, and Orientation

In their study of part-time faculty, Gappa and Leslie (1993) noted, "Recruitment and hiring set the tone for employment relations with part-time faculty because they are frequently the first contact between the institution and the part timer (or non-tenure-track faculty member)" (p. 145). Most studies agree that colleges have no formal or systemized process for recruitment or hiring and approach the hiring of non-tenure-track faculty very casually (Cross and Goldenberg, 2009; Gappa and Leslie, 1993). For example, many of the colleges in Gappa and Leslie's study (1993) had no formal criteria for the appointment of part-time faculty. Community colleges tended to have more standardized qualifications or criteria. Baldwin and Chronister (2001) noted that institutional policy documents do not set forth the minimum degree qualifications necessary for full-time non-tenure-track faculty appointments. Credentials and qualifications differed markedly by discipline and institution, with professional schools emphasizing work experience, for example. Some institutions seek experienced practitioners for non-tenure-track positions who bring vast experience, while others hold different criteria.

Baldwin and Chronister (2001) and Cross and Goldenberg (2009) found that administrators were not willing to conduct national searches and hiring processes equivalent or at least similar to tenure-track appointments because of the cost. Cross and Goldenberg (2009) and Gappa and Leslie (1993) suggest that local, spur-of-the-moment hiring is common. Yet this pattern may be changing for full-time non-tenure-track faculty over time; a recent study by Hollenshead and others (2007) found that more than half of administrators in a national study said they conduct formal searches for full-time non-tenure-track faculty similar to those for tenure-track hires. It appears this process may be formalizing more than in the past. Yet part-time employees continue to be hired through informal processes (Hollenshead and others, 2007). Hollenshead and others (2007) point out the irony that administrators put in so much more effort for tenure-track faculty or even full-time non-tenure-track faculty when on average their duration of employment is much the same—seven years for full-time non-tenure-track faculty and 5.5 years for part-timers.

If an institution has few formal criteria and invests little in the recruitment and hiring of non-tenure-track faculty, it is likely to obtain candidates who may not meet expectations—because those expectations have not been articulated publicly and communicated to candidates, not because the person is not well qualified. Many of the institutions Baldwin and Chronister (2001) studied hired individuals within days of the semester's starting. The short time frame between hiring and beginning work does not allow for any orientation socialization, or even preparation for the course. Part-time faculty who teach on a more ongoing basis and are in a pool for hiring each semester also received very late notice about teaching a course, typically days before class. Baldwin and Chronister (2001) did identify a few institutions that treated the hiring of full-time non-tenure-track faculty similar to their tenure-track colleagues. Geography played a role, however, with more isolated campuses having to conduct a more systematic and national or regional search, while urban institutions or institutions located where other colleges are nearby were less likely to conduct systematic hiring processes and extend the process regionally or nationally. Collective bargaining institutions had more detailed hiring processes, with the contract specifying posting requirements for positions and a timetable for hiring. A collective bargaining process may create a more intentional approach to recruitment and hiring. Gappa and Leslie (1993) also found no attention to affirmative action in the recruitment and appointment of non-tenure-track faculty.

Various studies have noted that non-tenure-track faculty (both part time and full time) are often excluded from orientation processes (Gappa and Leslie, 1993; Schell and Stock, 2001; Conley and Leslie, 2002). A limited set of institutions provide a handbook to non-tenure-track faculty or leave it up to department chairs to offer some welcome and socialization, which often does not occur (Baldwin and Chronister, 2001; Gappa and Leslie, 1993). Collectively, these studies suggest that non-tenure-track faculty are recruited, hired, and oriented haphazardly, which signals minimal institutional commitment and investment. We suspect that recruitment, hiring, and orientation differ by discipline and department; future studies may want to further investigate this issue.

Salary

Salary, benefits, and support services vary significantly between full-time and part-time contracts. Full-time non-tenure-track faculty generally have salaries closer to those of tenure-track faculty, enjoy similar benefits to tenure-track faculty, and are able to take advantage of professional development and other privileges and benefits (Hollenshead and others, 2007). These faculty are more likely to have regular salary adjustments and are sometimes part of a promotion and evaluation system. In Hollenshead and others' study, 71 percent of full-time non-tenure-track faculty received pay raises for good performance. Despite these trends, however, Curtis (2005) found that in general full-time non-tenure-track faculty make 26 percent less than tenured faculty.

The situation is more distinctive for part-time faculty, who are often ineligible for benefits, salary adjustments (given at only 50 percent of institutions in a national sample), promotion systems, or evaluation. Part-time faculty also make much less money than full-time non-tenure-track faculty—$7,978 for a course compared with $5,564 for a part-timer (Hollenshead and others, 2007). Another national study found that part-time faculty earn approximately 60 percent less than comparable full-time tenure-track faculty in institutional salary when expressed on an hourly basis (Curtis, 2005; Toutkoushian and Bellas, 2003).

In examining institutional differences for full-time non-tenure-track salary only, Baldwin and Chronister (2001) found that master's and baccalaureate institutions are likely to pay more comparable salaries to tenure-track and non-tenure-track faculty and to have similar qualifications, while research and doctoral institutions tend to pay their non-tenure-track faculty less than their tenure-track faculty. Additionally, public institutions pay lower salaries to full-time non-tenure-track faculty; private institutions are closer to comparable salary between tenure and non-tenure-track faculty. The reasons for the lower salaries varied from an oversupply of qualified candidates to some non-tenure-track faculty's having lesser qualifications.

Benefits

As noted, those non-tenure-track faculty who are full time actually have benefits similar to those on the tenure track. Similar to part-time workers in the business sector, however, the same cannot be said for part-time faculty. In a national study, only 51 percent of part-time faculty received some form of benefits—typically health benefits—but it was often not the same package of benefits given to full-time faculty, which included life insurance, retirement, and sick leave (Hollenshead and others, 2007). In fact, Gappa and Leslie (1993) discovered that institutions often do not rehire part-time faculty because they might become eligible for benefits if they have been working for the institution for a long and continuous period. Gappa and Leslie (1993) also found that many part-time faculty do not have written contracts in place, further limiting their claim to any institutional benefits. In their study, they discovered that institutions do not make information available about any benefits that do exist for part timers. They also found that part-time faculty were in fact unaware of benefits and would have used them if they had been informed.

Support Services

To be able to fulfill the responsibilities of a faculty member, faculty often rely on campus support services for various reasons ranging from materials such as paper and chalk to professional development. Campuses differ, however, as to whether they provide office space, supplies, equipment, and access to secretarial services for full-time and part-time non-tenure-track faculty. Full-time faculty generally have adequate support and services to conduct their work, but a variety of studies have demonstrated that part-time faculty have more limited access to office space, supplies and equipment, and secretarial support (Gappa and Leslie, 1993; Outcalt, 2002). The lack of support services may be related to other factors: with the lack of office space, part-time faculty may find it difficult to be on campus when they are not teaching, and because many teach classes during the evening, part-time faculty may not be able to use the support services available during regular work hours.

Professional Development

Although many institutions do not provide professional development, recognition has been growing of the importance of professional development for non-tenure-track faculty. Institutions are increasingly creating planned programs for developing and improving teaching effectiveness, which is the primary role of non-tenure-track faculty (Baldwin and Chronister, 2001). Less common is the opportunity for funding to travel for professional development or research (Baldwin and Chronister, 2001; Gappa and Leslie, 1993; Conley and Leslie, 2002). Professional development that is offered is also not aimed at furthering individuals but much more toward meeting institutional goals. This factor differs for tenure-track faculty, who can participate in conferences and professional development of their own choosing. Professional development opportunities are more commonly available for full-time non-tenure-track faculty than for part-time faculty (Baldwin and Chronister, 2001).

Job Security and Seniority

One area of shared experience between full-time and part-time non-tenure-track faculty is the issue of job security and seniority. In various surveys done by different union groups, job security is often named as one of the top three concerns of full- and part-time faculty (National Education Association, 2002; American Federation of Teachers, 2010). Because both appointment types are for a limited term, both groups of faculty worry about their term-to-term or year-to-year employment. Baldwin and Chronister (2001) found that one year was the most common contract length across all institutions for full-time non-tenure-track faculty. A limited number of institutions use multiyear contracts for full-time non-tenure-track appointments (Baldwin and Chronister, 2001). Renewal policies also vary, with 48 percent of the institutions Baldwin and Chronister (2001) surveyed indicating unlimited renewal for full-time non-tenure-track faculty. Forty-two percent, however, set a limit on the number of years a faculty member may remain employed on term contract status. The institutions that set limits were trying to prevent non-tenure-track faculty from obtaining de facto tenure status, or they were trying to ensure an influx of new faculty expertise. It is clear that these types of policies at almost 50 percent of the institutions would lead to concerns about job stability, as eventually they will need to find an alternative place of employment.

Given limitations in current survey research, it is unclear the degree to which multiyear contracts are being used, but given percentages in earlier sampling of institutions, it appears to be a relatively uncommon practice. Part-time faculty face even more vulnerability, as they are typically hired only for the semester and find out about reappointment only a few days before the semester begins (Gappa and Leslie, 1993). Faculty can find themselves trying to find new employment at another institution within days of the semester's beginning. Institutions with collective bargaining are more likely to have seniority provisions for part-time faculty in which over time they accrue status and are first to be hired back the next semester to teach an available course (Gappa and Leslie, 1993).

Gappa and Leslie (1993) note the myth that part-time (and non-tenure-track) faculty are fly-by-night people who want no institutional affiliation or commitment. A similar stereotype is that part-time faculty all work six or seven jobs and run from institution to institution. Although certainly some faculty fit both of these profiles, the vast majority of part-time and non-tenure-track faculty enjoy relative longevity—as long as the institution can afford to hire them back. Most institutions tend to keep on both full-time and part-time non-tenure-track faculty, and nonreappointment is less common (Gappa and Leslie, 1993; Conley and Leslie, 2002). This fact by no means suggests that part-time and full-time non-tenure-track faculty have any sense of job security or seniority but that an institutional pattern exists for them to be hired back. Non-tenure-track faculty also exhibit loyalty to continue working at institutions with which they have become affiliated.

Job Responsibilities and Expectations

Although working conditions affect experience, role definition does as well. Various studies suggest that collective bargaining helps non-tenure-track faculty to gain clarity about their role definition (Gappa and Leslie, 1993; Hollenshead and others, 2007; Rhoades and Maitland, 2008). The workload of non-tenure-track faculty is typically defined in terms of teaching, but issues such as office hours, class preparation, and communicating with students are often not made clear to non-tenure-track faculty who do not have collective bargaining agreements. Collective bargaining agreements have been effective in specifying job responsibilities in broad categories and making expectations clear. Studies have also found that non-tenure-track faculty may be asked to conduct administrative tasks, supervise clinical or fieldwork, train or mentor teaching assistants, or participate in service work without clarity about pay. Again, collective bargaining agreements are clear about what administrative or service work a non-tenure-track faculty member can be asked to engage in (Hollenshead and others, 2007).

Institutional type is also important in distinguishing roles for non-tenure-track faculty. Baldwin and Chronister (2001) found that full-time non-tenure-track faculty are primarily contracted to teach lower-division courses only—at research, doctoral, and master's institutions. At four-year undergraduate institutions, non-tenure-track faculty teach both upper- and lower-division courses. Four-year undergraduate institutions were also more likely to have fairly similar role expectations for non-tenure-track and tenure-eligible positions. The only conclusion that Baldwin and Chronister developed in their study of full-time non-tenure-track role definition is that a consistent definition does not exist. Role definition appears to depend on the mission, culture, and academic personnel needs of the institution.

Hollenshead and others' study (2007) reinforces this finding about inconsistent role definition, as some institutions reported expecting non-tenure-track faculty (both full and part time) to advise students, serve on committees, and even conduct research. In fact, full-time non-tenure-track faculty at four-year institutions were expected to advise and mentor students (63 percent), engage in committee work (51 percent), and create professional products or research (27 percent). So although role definition tends to focus on teaching, many institutions are sorting out their expectations for non-tenure-track faculty, and it appears they are expanding the range of areas that full-time non-tenure-track faculty are expected to work in overtime (Hollenshead and others' more recent study shows more variation than Baldwin and Chronister's study from 2001). And although some institutions expect this enlarged portfolio of work, they do not provide release time or a reduced teaching load for faculty to participate in advising, service, or the development of professional products or research. "Although institutions may provide space and reimburse certain costs for full-time non-tenure-track faculty, they do not by and large support such activities by providing the time to do so nor do they provide the incentive of increased compensation. For part-time non-tenure-track faculty the rewards are even fewer" (Hollenshead and others, 2007, p. 14). The trend of expanding workload suggests an area of growing concern for the future.

In terms of teaching load, full-time non-tenure-track faculty tend to have a larger teaching load than tenure-track faculty, but it varied by institution and discipline (Hollenshead and others, 2007). Non-tenure-track faculty at research and doctoral universities were likely to have heavier loads than master's and baccalaureate-level institutions (Baldwin and Chronister, 2001; Hollenshead and others, 2007; Schuster and Finkelstein, 2006). Moreover, the conditions of teaching are different for tenure-track and non-tenure-track faculty. Tenure-track faculty often receive teaching assistants to help with coursework, particularly large courses, but non-tenure-track faculty are expected to take on the burden of a course without any teaching assistants. They often teach courses such as composition or math that have significant amounts of grading or lower-division classes with a higher number of enrollments per class. Faculty in a qualitative study of full-time non-tenure-track faculty in English described their teaching loads as extremely high, often brutal, and found they worked significantly more hours than they were compensated for (Shaker, 2008).

The ability of non-tenure-track faculty to participate in curriculum development varies tremendously based on their contract type. Full-time non-tenure-track faculty are sometimes included in designing new courses or building new curricula and are able to design their own courses (Baldwin and Chronister, 2001). Part-time faculty are less likely to be given opportunities for curriculum development and are more likely to be given standard curriculum to teach (Gappa and Leslie, 1993). Disciplinary differences also are likely to exist but have not been examined in any detail. For example, we imagine that professional areas might allow more input from non-tenure-track faculty because they respect their expertise. We hypothesize that the liberal arts is an area where non-tenure-track faculty may have less direct involvement in the development and creation of curriculum.

Unfortunately, the role of non-tenure-track faculty has often become an accumulation of activities and tasks that tenure-track faculty are not interested in doing: teaching lower-division courses, overseeing teaching assistants, and program administration (Hollenshead and others, 2007). This factor may be one of the reasons that Burgan (2006) notes tenured faculty have been silent about the growth of non-tenure-track faculty. Baldwin and Chronister (2001) note that what is clear is that no consensus has emerged on appropriate workload or role definition for full-time non-tenure-track faculty. The role definition of full-time non-tenure-track faculty appears to be whatever the immediate needs are of departments, and they can vary tremendously in and across institutions. The full-time non-tenure-track faculty role is constantly expanding and changing to meet institutional needs. It looks increasingly similar to tenure-track faculty responsibilities in terms of the diversity of the role but with the most unfortunate conditions or aspects of the role—monotonous and large classes, poorly scheduled times, and service and administrative work tenured faculty do not want to do (Baldwin and Chronister, 2001; Hollenshead and others, 2007).

This ever-expanding role definition for full-time non-tenure-track faculty leads to unclear expectations or understanding of what a non-tenure-track job might involve, and it may lead to dissatisfaction for the employee. The overall picture appears to be that the role definition is changing over time and that more tension is being created between the definition and expectations—which are often larger than the written contracts. Part-time faculty roles may also be changing, but equal attention has not been paid in recent years to documenting the role expectations of part-time faculty.

Perspective on Faculty Life

Although we know a lot about the working conditions of non-tenure-track faculty, we know much less about how they experience these conditions. And although anecdotal accounts exist of non-tenure-track faculty (notably, *The Chronicle of Higher Education* publishes a column about the experiences of non-tenure-track faculty), very little systematic research actually exists about their own experiences. Gappa and Leslie (1993) and Baldwin and Chronister (2001) spoke to part-time and full-time non-tenure-track faculty in their case studies but did not collect systematic data. One of the most comprehensive national datasets about non-tenure-track faculty (Tuckman, 1978) was commissioned by the AAUP, is significantly out of date, and mostly examines satisfaction and work conditions. Many studies on the topic tend to start with administrators and their perceptions and decisions and then shift to non-tenure-track faculty. Hollenshead and others (2007) note this gap in the literature and explain the importance of hearing the voices of non-tenure-track faculty themselves. The best way to truly develop a path forward is to understand their experiences with these working conditions.

This section shares some of the voices about the experiences of non-tenure-track faculty from the limited studies that have been conducted; more research is needed that directly involves non-tenure-track faculty. In fact, a movement in the non-tenure-track ranks is the importance of non-tenure-track faculty conducting their own research and voicing their concerns, because current studies (done typically by tenure-track faculty) have at times misunderstood their experiences or framed a study in a way that does not capture the complexity or true issues. A collection of essays by faculty in composition is one example of research by non-tenure-track faculty themselves (Schell and Stock, 2001). One of the challenges to conducting such research is getting non-tenure-track (particularly part-time) faculty to return surveys or participate in studies. The recent CAW survey developed and administered by non-tenure-track faculty actually has received a large response rate and thousands of non-tenure-track faculty have participated. The AFT (American Federation of Teachers, 2010) recently conducted a national phone survey of non-tenure-track faculty and experienced difficulty obtaining responses, as many of the faculty were part time and have multiple job responsibilities. We should also note that tenure-track faculty can develop sound research on non-tenure-track faculty, but we also believe additional insight is likely garnered from some research conducted by non-tenure-track faculty. This section highlights some of the insights garnered from non-tenure-track faculty who are involved in research, either through their own works or with other faculty.

Hostile Climate

Studies of non-tenure-track faculty have identified that they often experience a negative climate among colleagues that at best is disrespectful or dismissive and at worst hostile. Several studies of the experience of part-time faculty suggest that tenure-track faculty express antagonism toward part-time non-tenure-track faculty (Gappa and Leslie, 1993; Leslie, Kellams, and Gunne, 1982). Furthermore, full-time non-tenure-track faculty often express animosity toward part-time faculty, whom they feel they compete with for courses and job security (Kezar and Sam, 2009). The groups are not only in a class system where certain groups receive a more privileged place in the hierarchy but also actively express tension between subgroups (some of these tensions are addressed in Kezar and Sam, 2010b), making the climate uncomfortable. In a recent interview study of full-time and part-time non-tenure-track faculty leaders, the same animosity was expressed between groups as of 2009, so the hostile climates are not diminishing from studies conducted in the early 1990s, even as their numbers rise precipitously (Kezar and Sam, 2009). People have speculated about why animosity exists, but no national studies have been conducted. Evidence from case studies of campuses suggests that tenure-track faculty perceive non-tenure-track faculty as a threat to the institution of tenure, have lesser qualifications and are worse teachers, affect the collegial environment of departments, and lower the educational quality of the institution (Baldwin and Chronister, 2001; Cross and Goldenberg, 2009; Gappa and Leslie, 1993). One would hypothesize that this hostile climate affects the ability to develop collegial relationships and work effectively with others, yet these hypotheses need to be tested.

Two-Class System

This hostile climate is also connected to what non-tenure-track faculty experience as a two-class system: nontenure track and tenure track faculty. As Baldwin and Chronister (2001) suggest, "Although the experience of full-time non-tenure-track faculty varies considerably by disciplinary field and institution of employment, as a general rule these members of the academic profession occupy a disadvantaged status when compared to their tenured and tenure eligible colleagues. Whether the issue is workload, compensation, professional development, or support, full-time faculty on term contracts are usually in a less favorable situation than their tenure class counterpart" (p. 7). However, many studies have noted that a three-class system—part time, full-time nontenure track, and tenure track or tenured—is emerging in American higher education.

The first distinction is whether a faculty member is part-time or full-time nontenure track. Part-time faculty, as noted in previous sections of this chapter, have worse working conditions and are often seen as even more peripheral and outside the norm of tenure-track faculty. The next factor that shapes the experience of non-tenure-track faculty in this three-class system is their desires and motivations, as described by Maynard and Joseph (2008). Baldwin and Chronister (2001) examined differences among full-time non-tenure-track faculty—tenure-track hopefuls, tenure-track rejecters, and alternative or second-career faculty (they also looked at accompanying spouses, but their experiences were similar to others listed here). The major difference among these groups is that faculty who desire a tenure-track appointment are less likely to believe that their experience is positive and register more concern about the second-class citizenship. We summarize Baldwin and Chronister's findings (2001) in more detail, as they highlight a key point in our synthesis of the literature: experience depends on motivation and other individual factors.

Tenure-track hopefuls were extremely frustrated by the two-tier system and felt that the longer they stayed in the non-tenure-track tier (which they perceive to be lower), the less likely they would be marketable and ever able to obtain a tenure-track position. Research demonstrates that these concerns have some merit, as only about one-third of non-tenure-track faculty transfer into tenure-track positions (Hollenshead and others, 2007; Schuster and Finkelstein, 2006). The heavy teaching loads that they carry make it difficult to do any scholarly work, which would make them more eligible for tenure-track positions. They also worry because they know that at many institutions they cannot stay for their entire career and are always worried about where their next move will be. For example, some institutions hire full-time non-tenure-track faculty as visiting professors, but if they are still employed in the same capacity after three years they must be considered for the tenure track. Institutions often choose not to renew the faculty member's contract after the third year.

Tenure-track rejecters had observed the tenure-track path and decided that they would like to pursue a non-tenure-track path because they felt it would better able them to pursue their interests, whether teaching or a more balanced lifestyle (Baldwin and Chronister, 2001; Gappa, Austin, and Trice, 2007; Outcalt, 2002). As a result, they were often happy with the general orientation of their role but still registered concerns about the second-class citizenship. They had no desire to change the nature of their role, but they were concerned about the two-tier system, which was apparent to them in their day-to-day work lives.

Alternative or second-career faculty were often more concentrated in professional fields; they join the faculty as a result of retirement, the need for new challenges, or disaffection with the previous career. Individuals who were close to retirement or were disaffected from another career were often satisfied with their work experience and were not looking for permanent employment or career progression (Conley and Leslie, 2002). The second-class status was of little concern to them. They were not interested in participating in governance, professional development, and even salary differences, for they approach the position as a hobby rather than a career. Some second-career faculty desired a tenure-track appointment and only took the non-tenure-track appointment because they felt they could eventually move into a tenure-track appointment. These faculty were disappointed with the second-class citizenship. Motivation heavily affects experience (Baldwin and Chronister, 2001). These same motivations can also be examined for part-time faculty, and similar differences would likely be identified.

Upsides of Non-Tenure-Track Faculty Work

Studies suggest that although the non-tenure-track faculty role has many negative or difficult aspects (which have received the majority of research attention), some positive aspects also exist (Baldwin and Chronister, 2001; Shaker, 2008). Although they are managed professionals, non-tenure-track faculty acknowledged that their positions allow them flexibility and freedom in hours and days of work, including having summers off (Shaker, 2008). As committed professionals, they want to learn on an ongoing basis and to engage in professional development. They appreciated that the faculty role requires them to keep up on reading in their field and that the institution offers professional development options (Shaker, 2008). Faculty reflected that working with students, being in a helping profession, and being connected to a discipline and subject that they love were rewarding. In a qualitative study of eighteen full-time non-tenure-track faculty, Shaker (2008) found that they believed that the position was perfect for them: it allowed them to teach, work with students, and work with their discipline without the pressure of tenure-track demands, particularly publishing for academic venues. These faculty could write for lay audiences or more practical or creative purposes without the pressure to produce academic writing for journals. It is important to add in these positive aspects of the non-tenure-track faculty experience as well. Although there are fewer direct policy-related recommendations, this research does help to understand their motivations and attitudes. We now move on to satisfaction and commitment that are typical measures for understanding how their experience shapes their attitudes.

Satisfaction

The common mythology is that part-time faculty are strongly dissatisfied with their jobs and feel exploited given the poor working conditions, hostile climate, and unclear role definition that we have documented (no major studies have been conducted on full-time non-tenure-track faculty, so this section is aimed at part-time faculty). The key to understanding this myth is the concept of person-job fit. One of the more confusing findings of studies is that part-time faculty tend to be more satisfied than or as satisfied as their tenure-track colleagues (Antony and Valdez, 2002; Conley and Leslie, 2002; Toutkoushian and Bellas, 2003; Outcalt, 2002; Schuster and Finkelstein, 2006). This finding emerges repeatedly in various national studies (American Federation of Teachers, 2010). Studies suggest that part-time faculty are more satisfied with their workload and personal control over their professional time, allowing a more balanced work life (Antony and Valdez, 2002). The heterogeneity of the part-time faculty once again helps to explain this confusing outcome. The typology already described of part-time faculty suggests that many individuals choose part-time or non-tenure-track positions because of the flexibility they offer or their life circumstances, because they already have a full-time job and desire to teach, or because they have retired. Closer analysis has demonstrated, however, that although non-tenure-track faculty are satisfied overall, they are less satisfied than tenure-track faculty with regard to salary, benefits, job security, or time to keep current in their field (Benjamin, 1998).

Maynard and Joseph (2008) note that the key element of satisfaction is whether a person desires full-time work; if they desire full-time work but only part-time work is available to them, then they will be less satisfied. In their study, they examined the job satisfaction of three different groups of faculty: full-time faculty, part-time faculty preferring a part-time position, and part-time faculty preferring a full-time position. Involuntary part-time faculty were least satisfied with their compensation, job security, and opportunities for advancement. Voluntary part-time faculty and full-time faculty reported similar levels of satisfaction on these three areas compared with full-time faculty. Their findings highlight the need to continue to disaggregate data related to part-time and full-time non-tenure-track faculty to truly understand their experiences and satisfaction. The study also suggests the need for further study of non-tenure-track faculty because their perceptions about their work were critical in explaining many of the confusing and conflicting research findings that have emerged (Maynard and Joseph, 2008). In a study of a single community college, Jacoby (2006) demonstrated that part-time faculty who wanted full-time tenure-track work were also dissatisfied and that the key difference to understanding satisfaction was a person's perceptions or desires about employment.

Related to person-job-fit theory is the concept of career stage. Feldman and Turnley (2001) demonstrated that late-career part-time faculty had more positive job attitudes and satisfaction than early-career faculty. This finding highly correlates to the last set of studies on voluntary versus involuntary part-time status. Early-career faculty tend to be interested in full-time positions and maintain part-time work involuntarily. The sources of satisfaction for early-career faculty included scheduling flexibility, their coworkers, job autonomy, work challenge, and quality of supervision. Pay, fringe benefits, and advancement opportunities were rated much lower in terms of satisfaction. Faculty late in their career registered high job satisfaction, professional commitments, and organizational citizenship. Meanwhile, faculty in their early careers noted that they felt less satisfaction and commitment and much more job deprivation. Midcareer faculty described both positive and negative aspects of their part-time positions. Although this study was conducted of only one university, it reinforces a trend that appears to be emerging in the data about factors that shape satisfaction.

Additionally, studies demonstrate that the satisfaction of part-time faculty varies by discipline or field of study and gender. The most satisfied individuals come from professional or vocational fields, the most dissatisfied from liberal arts fields (Benjamin, 2002). These findings are interpreted to mean that individuals in professional fields are likely to have additional full-time jobs and are less dependent on their faculty positions for salary and benefits. In addition, the professional fields tend to have climates that respect non-tenure-track faculty more, which may affect their satisfaction. Faculty in the liberal arts are half as likely to say they were interested in a full-time position, while vocational faculty prefer working on a part-time basis. Women are less satisfied than men on three measures of satisfaction, including overall job satisfaction, satisfaction with benefits, and satisfaction with salary (Toutkoushian and Bellas, 2003).

Although institutional differences have not been examined in relationship to satisfaction, the difference in working conditions at some institutions (for example baccalaureate and master's schools that allow faculty to teach upper-division courses) might also suggest some differences in satisfaction by institutional type that need to be researched in the future. A study specifically looking at community college faculty (Outcalt, 2002) found that full-time faculty were more satisfied than part-time faculty, which contrasts with earlier findings from the 1970s and 1980s, where part-time faculty were equally satisfied or more satisfied than full-time faculty. The difference between full-time and part-time faculty, however, was nominal.

The same study suggests that part-time faculty feel less stress on the job. Outcalt (2002) suggests that this finding "contradicts popular wisdom that part-time faculty, with their sometimes makeshift and patched together schedules, inevitably suffer from more workplace stress than their full-time counterparts" (p. 81). Moreover, the more involved they were on campus with professional development and instruction, orientation, departmental affairs, and service, the more satisfied both part-time and full-time faculty were, which suggests that involvement in the life of the campus leads to satisfaction. O'Meara, Terosky, and Neumann (2008) posit that the number of non-tenure-track faculty on the campus might also affect satisfaction and the perception of non-tenure-track faculty. If a campus has 60 or 70 percent non-tenure-track faculty for a long time, non-tenure-track faculty may be more likely to be satisfied because policies are in place or because they have gained greater respect from other members of the institution. Campuses where the number of non-tenure-track faculty recently increased, however, may experience more dissatisfaction among all faculty as they adjust to new conditions without changes in institutional structures and culture. Thus, a dizzying array of factors and conditions influence part-time and full-time faculty satisfaction.

Commitment

One of the few studies of non-tenure-track faculty examines commitment levels; it found that part-time faculty reported higher emotional commitment to the institution than full-time faculty (Maynard and Joseph, 2008). The authors offer no explanation for this finding and note that it is unexpected because part-time faculty are not provided the same social and technical support that permanent and full-time employees receive. They hypothesize that part of the strong commitment may be related to their generally strong satisfaction. This finding about commitment is extremely important, because various researchers (Jaeger and Eagan, 2009; Umbach, 2007) hypothesize that non-tenure-track faculty lack commitment to the institution, resulting in poorer outcomes for students. They use social exchange and social capital theories (Kezar and Sam, 2010b) to explain the lesser commitments of faculty without ever actually measuring faculty commitment levels. We need further study regarding commitment, as Maynard and Joseph's study used a small sample.

Concerns and Unmet Expectations

Thus far, we have examined the working conditions of non-tenure-track faculty and perspectives of faculty life. In this section we examine specific concerns and unmet needs and expectations they describe, which sometimes overlap with the poor working conditions we described earlier. They also note, however, issues beyond working conditions or the campus climate. It is important to understand these concerns, as Shaker (2008) found that campuses that address issues like inconsistent policy implementation, salary, governance, promotion, and job security had faculty that felt much better about the institution in terms of trust, security, and morale. Moreover, research from business suggests that companies that address concerns of contingent and part-time workers and set up effective policies have much stronger organizational outcomes (Arnold, Cooper, and Robertson, 1995). Research presented here is on the documented concerns of non-tenure-track faculty rather than hypothesized concerns that can be inferred from examining working conditions alone.

Salary and Job Security
Gappa and Leslie (1993) and Baldwin and Chronister (2001) did not systematically survey the faculty but did identify through their interviews a deep concern about job security for a number of non-tenure-track faculty, again

ones who depend on their faculty jobs as their primary source of employment or income. Salary was also of greatest concern when this work was the primary employment rather than a secondary income.

Governance

Gappa and Leslie (1993) noted part-timers' anger and frustration about exclusion from collegial activities and career opportunities. One of the major areas where part-timers expressed concern was their lack of involvement in decision making and governance. The inability to have input for courses that they spent a great deal of time teaching or designing professional development programs was a source of frustration. Part-time faculty have been consistently shown to be excluded from governance at institutions (Hollenshead and others, 2007). Part-time faculty are often not allowed to attend departmental or institutional meetings. Baldwin and Chronister (2001) found that full-time non-tenure-track faculty are more actively involved in governance, with about 50 percent of their sample institutions allowing them to participate in the faculty senate and other forms of governance and 75 percent being allowed to participate in departmental affairs. The researchers note that although restrictions exist on formal governance, many non-tenure-track faculty noted their involvement in informal governance such as more local decisions or being asked informally for their advice.

Anderson (2002), Baldwin and Chronister (2001), and Shaker (2008) all found that some full-time non-tenure-track faculty were happy *not* to be expected to participate in governance and were content to leave it to the tenure-track faculty because they perceived it as a waste of time or lacking meaning. Consistently, though, non-tenure-track faculty (both part time and full time) registered concern about not having input on decisions that directly affect them. Yet this trend appears to be changing. Hollenshead and others (2007) found that 78 percent of full-time non-tenure-track faculty could participate in the academic senate and 95 percent were included in departmental affairs, a substantial increase from Baldwin and Chronister (2001). Part-time non-tenure-track faculty remained more excluded than full-time non-tenure-track faculty, but they also were included more than in the past, with 35 percent of part-time faculty having the ability to participate in the senate and 66 percent being able to participate in departmental affairs.

Increased participation rights, however, do not necessarily mean voice or power on campus. On campuses where non-tenure-track faculty are allowed to participate, they are often not given voting rights or only given partial voting rights (Kezar and Sam, 2010a). They are also typically given token status. For example, they might be allowed to have two members on the faculty senate that has more than ninety individuals, or they are the single member of a twenty-member committee (Kezar and Sam, 2010a). In all these circumstances, they recognize they have limited or no voice in the institution to raise concerns about teaching and learning. Involvement in governance has been related to some important outcomes. For example, Pisani and Stott (1998) found that integration into the department and decision making was the strongest predictor of a part-time faculty member's motivation to commit to more in-depth student advising. In addition, through governance non-tenure-track faculty can affect other conditions of their working conditions such as benefits or orientation. Baldwin and Chronister's overall impression of governance (2001) is that the vast majority of campuses they visited casually neglect this issue.

Inconsistent Policy

Across a variety of studies, a major concern noted by non-tenure-track faculty is the inconsistency in the application of policies. Gappa and Leslie (1993) describe a multitude of policies for part-time faculty that are inconsistently applied in institutions: hiring processes, orientation, participation in governance, contract terms, salary, evaluation, promotion, and other working conditions that vary from department to department and sometimes even from person to person—raising concerns about equity. Baldwin and Chronister (2001) describe a situation in which full-time non-tenure-track faculty on three- and five-year contracts had a new department chair who changed their appointments to one-year contracts. Because no standards or set policies exist, policies can be changed at a whim. Baldwin and Chronister use the words of a full-time non-tenure-track faculty member who begged for clarity and consistency in policy and practices to illustrate this concern: "The institution has to clarify the non-tenure-track status for us and treat us fairly. What are the parameters within which we walk?" (p. 47). At present we have no data to understand how widespread the issue of inconsistent policy implementation is. We assume that over time, campuses will become more systematic in their approaches.

Teaching Restrictions

Another major concern for non-tenure-track faculty is the circumscribed nature of teaching, whereby they have little input into curriculum design and implementation. The lack of input into the creation of curriculum and syllabus, textbook selection, or decisions affected their morale, status, and efficacy as a professional (Baldwin and Chronister, 2001). Moreover, they are often restricted from teaching upper-division courses, which leads to monotonous teaching of the same course multiple times during a semester or year. By not teaching upper-division courses, they are often not able to keep up to date with changes in the field and be challenged by students as they mature and can ask more complex questions. Non-tenure-track faculty feel they are falling behind in professional knowledge that is important to their success and rejuvenation.

Evaluation

Various studies have identified "diverse, sometimes erratic, approaches to evaluating" the performance of non-tenure-track faculty as a major concern (Baldwin and Chronister, 2001, p. 65). Baldwin and Chronister (2001) identified how institutions hire full-time non-tenure-track faculty to teach a variety of lower-division courses but evaluate them on the same criteria as tenure-track faculty, with expectations for research and service. Other institutions used only student evaluations of teaching rather than creating a more diverse portfolio, which could adequately capture the faculty member's performance. These researchers found that most of the full-time non-tenure-track faculty were concerned about the validity of review procedures and the institution's evaluation criteria (Baldwin and Chronister, 2001). Having a fair evaluation system is important because it guarantees that data are collected about performance—and as long as individuals are strong performers, it makes not rehiring much more difficult. Collective bargaining agreements often do not include evaluation processes or strictly limit their use and function, however (Gappa and

Leslie, 1993). Collective bargaining processes tend to be less favorable or trusting of administrators' use of the evaluations and therefore tend to deemphasize this process (Rhoades, 1998). We need more up-to-date data and systematic research to better understand the scope of this problem.

Contract Renewal

A major concern of non-tenure-track faculty is the time frame under which the institution provides notification of contract renewal. Some faculty are given only a month or two weeks' notice before the next academic year, making it extremely difficult to find another full-time appointment in that short time frame (Baldwin and Chronister, 2001; Rhoades and Maitland, 2008). Researchers found, however, that most institutions follow the AAUP's provisions for contract renewal for full-time non-tenure-track faculty, which stipulates three months' notice in the first year, six months' notice in the second year, and one year's notice for individuals teaching three or more years (Baldwin and Chronister, 2001; Hollenshead and others, 2007). Hollenshead and others (2007) found that two out of five part-time faculty are given a month or less notice, suggesting that renewal notification is even more precarious for part-time faculty.

Promotion

Although some institutions provide a career path and progression for full-time non-tenure-track faculty, it appears about 50 percent (perhaps less) have not established a career ladder. Fifty percent of campuses sampled by Baldwin and Chronister (2001) had some provision to allow for long-term employment by full-time non-tenure-track faculty, with career progression and some ability for promotion. Some institutions use rankings similar to those for tenure-track faculty and have non-tenure-track faculty move through the ranks of assistant, associate, and full professor. Other institutions have simpler tracks such as lecturer and senior lecturer. Certainly for institutions that have a time limit on how long a non-tenure-track faculty member can be employed, having a promotion scheme may not make sense. Part-time faculty also commonly lack titles, ranks, or promotional opportunities to distinguish individual careers from one another at a given institution (Gappa and Leslie, 1993; Outcalt,

2002). Though complaints about the lack of distinction and promotion are not ubiquitous, a large proportion of part-time community college faculty expressed dissatisfaction (Conley and Leslie, 2002). Non-tenure-track faculty, particularly full-time faculty, believed promotional schemes should be put in place, which would enhance their contributions to campus.

Academic Freedom

The AAUP issued reports in 1986 and 1993 about the status of non-tenure-track faculty, which raised a variety of concerns already noted in studies of non-tenure-track faculty, including job security and inequitable compensation. The AAUP, however, also raised a concern that is often not raised in studies of non-tenure-track faculty: academic freedom. Although a limited amount of evidence or number of research studies provide specific evidence for this concern, reports in the media from time to time note non-tenure-track faculty who have been fired for saying something critical of the institution. Because the AAUP has represented many non-tenure-track faculty in these cases, its involvement and experience may suggest that this situation is another area of concern. Baldwin and Chronister (2001) noted that some full-time non-tenure-track faculty expressed concern about academic freedom—not in relationship to teaching and scholarship but related to shared governance or saying something critical about the administration. The researchers found that overall, academic freedom appears to be respected on most campuses they visited.

Most part-time faculty find themselves very satisfied with the level of academic freedom in their institutions (American Federation of Teachers, 2010; Conley and Leslie, 2002). The idea of academic freedom in the classroom versus in the institution may be conflated, however. Most part-time faculty felt that their autonomy and academic freedom in the classroom were protected, with little oversight. On the flip side, numerous non-tenure-track faculty, part time included, noted that they often did not have a voice in the institution or did not want to speak for fear it would jeopardize their employment (Gappa and Leslie, 1993; Kezar and Sam, 2009; Gappa, Austin, and Trice, 2007). Thus, the present evidence is mixed. Rather than just an institutional policy issue, many argue that academic freedom is covered by First Amendment protections (see Euben, 2002).

Tenure-Track Restrictions

A major concern for individuals who desire a tenure-track position is policies that enable or prohibit non-tenure-track faculty from moving into tenure-track positions. Currently, only 5 percent of institutions sampled nationally have policies that prohibit non-tenure-track faculty from moving into tenure-track positions (Hollenshead and others, 2007). On the other hand, only 23 percent have policies that permit such activity. It appears that generally very few policies and procedures are in place to encourage this type of recruitment. Research suggests that institutional type also affects movement between non-tenure-track and tenure-track positions, with doctoral extensive universities and liberal arts baccalaureate colleges reporting that moves do not frequently happen. Doctoral intensive universities and general baccalaureate colleges, however, are more likely to witness movement between non-tenure-track and tenure-track appointments. This trend is important for non-tenure-track faculty to know if they are interested in moving between positions. A related trend is for part-time faculty who want to move to full-time positions. National surveys show that close to 35 percent of part-time faculty want to move to full-time positions, which varies by institutional type (Schuster and Finkelstein, 2006). Some institutions provide provisions and encouragement for part-time faculty to apply for full-time positions, but national data suggest that much less movement from part time to full time occurs than for full time to tenure track. About a third of full-time non-tenure-track faculty who want to move to a tenure-track position make the transition.

Given all these concerns and the fact that unionized non-tenure-track faculty receive better pay, are offered a wider array of benefits, and have generally better working conditions, it would seem likely that non-tenure-track faculty will unionize in the future. A national study found, however, that 97 percent of four-year institutions report no unionizing activity on their campuses (Hollenshead and others, 2007).

Conclusion

This chapter helps the reader to understand the life and experiences of non-tenure-track faculty. Data suggest that working conditions are quite poor i many areas, ranging from recruiting practices to lack of promotion. The data on working conditions suggest that full-time non-tenure-track faculty have much better working conditions than their part-time counterparts, and the data suggest areas that may need attention on campuses. Yet the data alone cannot tell us whether full-time non-tenure-track faculty are more satisfied with their positions or more committed. Research on the perspective of non-tenure-track faculty about campus life suggests that they are fairly satisfied and committed (both full-time and part-time faculty) in general but that their experience declines when asked about specific working conditions. The general satisfaction and commitment can be explained by the various upsides that non-tenure-track faculty note about their experiences. Yet they universally feel like second-class citizens in a caste system. Non-tenure-track faculty have a vast array of concerns, but how widespread these concerns are is largely unknown, as no national data exist. All of these areas (working conditions, climate, and concerns) are constantly evolving, making it difficult to pinpoint the experience. The concerns overlap with working conditions but also move beyond them to other areas. The general point made throughout this chapter is that even though we are trying to summarize some basic patterns that vary by full- and part-time faculty, such a task will always be prone to lack of precision, as working conditions vary by discipline, climate depends on personal motivation and a desire for a tenure-track position, and concerns differ based on the type of institution. Campuses and departments need to conduct their own assessments of working conditions, climates, and concerns.

Plans of Action and Promising Policies

> Most students in higher education are being taught by tempo-
> rary laborers. Higher education as we have known it in the
> United States is gone. It is, however, reclaimable. To do so, we
> must move—quickly, together.
>
> —Jacobsohn, 2001, p. 183

LIKE THOSE OF MIGRANT WORKERS, the needs of non-tenure-track faculty have been generally ignored, and although various scholars and unions have promoted plans of action, little progress has been made in the past twenty-five years (Kezar and Sam, 2009). We feel that the landscape has changed in recent years; although it is difficult to know why, various factors seem to be improving the chances for action: the number of non-tenure-track faculty has reached a tipping point, academic unions are now actively organizing non-tenure-track faculty, other unions (such as the Communications Workers of America and the United Electrical, Radio and Machine Workers of America) are reaching out to non-tenure-track faculty, non-tenure-track faculty themselves are showing more activism, and recent attention by the media has focused attention on the group. This chapter examines four main topics related to plans of action and promising polices: (1) broad recommendations to address the issue of academic staffing; (2) specific practices and policies that support non-tenure-track faculty professionalization and success; (3) context-based solutions for making change; and (4) ways to achieve these needed changes. Although other authors have offered plans of action, our contribution to this topic is a summary of plans and new ideas about developing context-based solutions and novel ways to achieve plans of action that occur more from the bottom up.

Before reviewing these four areas relevant to improving academic staffing in the academy, it is important to review a few underlying assumptions that guide our thinking. We echo Gappa and Leslie's (1993) call for the importance of intentionality in any plan moving forward to staff the academy. Baldwin and Chronister (2001) similarly register concern, as their research demonstrates that institutions treat non-tenure-track faculty as short-term solutions, expendable and easily replaced, even though the institutions have long-term needs. Intentionality is simply missing. Instead of incorporating non-tenure-track faculty in thoughtful, meaningful ways that look toward the institutions' long-term goals, colleges and universities seem to take a reactive approach to non-tenure-track faculty—responding to immediate demands and fluctuations. Many research studies have noted that policies and practices related to non-tenure-track faculty are ad hoc, inconsistent, and perhaps even chaotic (Baldwin and Chronister, 2001; Gappa and Leslie, 1993). For example, many non-tenure-track faculty mention getting their class assignments only days before the first class begins, limiting preparation time (Gappa and Leslie, 1993). Having extremely decentralized campuses with no overall mandate to plan the use of part-time faculty is often an obstacle to planned use.

Planned use of faculty does not necessarily mean strong central decision making or control. It does mean, however, communication and a shared culture or understanding about appropriate numbers, hiring processes, socialization, and policies related to part-time or non-tenure-track faculty. This goal is often furthered through an academic staffing plan (discussed later in this chapter). Our approach differs from that of Gappa and Leslie (1993), who view the major responsibility for planning, controlling, and managing non-tenure-track faculty beginning with the top level of the institution. Instead, we call on the faculty (tenure track and nontenure track) to work with the administration to develop an appropriate staffing proposal for campuses. We suggest that the faculty bring their educational goals and curriculum plans and that administrators bring budget information and data. Previously, the planning and deployment of non-tenure-track faculty generally occurred with minimal input from tenure-track faculty and no input from non-tenure-track faculty, who also need to be included in planning. We also differ in that we do not depend on the administration for change; instead, we call for collective responsibility.

We offer one perspective and critique that relates to broad directions—the corporatization of the academy, also termed "academic capitalism" (Slaughter and Rhoades, 2004). Many scholars suggest that no progress can be made or faculty and working conditions improved until the overall corporatization of the academy is addressed. Sociological theories document a shift in the academy toward a neoliberal philosophy and approach to campus operations (more detail on this concept is provided in Kezar and Sam, 2010b). Slaughter and Rhoades (2004) suggest that unless this neoliberal logic is thoroughly questioned and the practices changed—such as outsourcing, non-tenure-track labor, reduction in instructional costs, rise in administrative costs—then smaller changes to professionalize the non-tenure-track faculty will not work, as the system is established to maximize profits rather than focused on creating the best learning environment. Thus, all the suggested directions made in this chapter are questionable, as they may not aim broadly enough or deeply enough to create the type of change needed to uproot corporatization. Slaughter and Rhoades (2004) would suggest that the plan of action most needed is to dismantle the corporate ideology that has taken hold on many campuses.

We now move to discuss differing views about the ways to move forward in staffing the academy, if leaders believe this is the direction that they should take (rather than dismantling the corporatization of campuses). These ideas are largely ideological, but some draw on theories presented in the chapter applied to the study of non-tenure-track faculty.

Broad Recommendations for Future Directions

The next section reviews detailed policies and practices that have been suggested for improving the working conditions and experiences of non-tenure-track faculty. Moving toward best practices suggests a specific plan of action or direction, however, and the literature notes several broad recommendations that should be considered before moving to specific policies. These recommendations speak to competing and sometimes complementary directions.

Interestingly, researchers currently tend to conceptualize non-tenure-track faculty as employees, not professionals, but their recommendations for the future treat non-tenure-track faculty as professionals.

Convert to Tenure Track over Time

A recommendation that stays closest to the traditional approach to staffing in the academy (maintaining a largely tenure-track faculty) is the conversion of non-tenure-track faculty to tenure-eligible tracks over time as it becomes financially feasible. This conversion also makes it possible to reach the ratios or quotas noted next. AAUP authors focus on the issue of conversion for full-time non-tenure-track faculty but also suggest that part-time faculty who are interested in full-time work should be given the opportunity for tenure-eligible positions; they also recommend that part-time positions be made tenure eligible. The argument made is that tenure is necessary to effectively meet the teaching and research mission of the institution and to attract the best men and women to the professoriate (Benjamin, 2002; Burgan, 2006). Tenure also provides a common set of professional values, standards, and responsibilities. Non-tenure-track faculty are largely not hired under these assumptions, nor are they socialized into common professional values. A recent report from the AAUP (2009) suggests that long-term contracts for non-tenure-track faculty are not sufficient and that conversion to tenure-track appointments is preferred. Therefore, institutions should convert faculty on non-tenure-track lines to eligibility for tenure positions, with only minor changes in job descriptions. Thus, if non-tenure-track faculty are primarily in teaching roles, they should obtain tenure-eligible positions where their focus is teaching (and vice versa if they are on a research-focused non-tenure-track line).

Set Tenure or Faculty Appointment Quotas

Another suggested path forward that has been promoted largely by unions is to develop quotas or ratios for tenure-track to non-tenure-track faculty. Collective bargaining agreements have begun to create and set ratios of tenured to non-tenure-track faculty and part-time to full-time faculty. The AFT has recommended that states adopt a policy that makes institutions obligated to have 75 percent of their faculty tenure track and no more than 25 percent nontenure track to preserve the traditional academic value system and the institution of tenure (American Federation of Teachers, 2005; Baldwin and Chronister, 2001). The establishment of tenure quotas at institutions may also alleviate any tension among the different faculty appointment groups. For example, full-time non-tenure-track faculty may not feel that their jobs are being threatened by part-time faculty positions if an established quota is in place. Some states (California, for example) have created policies related to the percentage of tenure-track faculty or the ratio of tenure to non-tenure-track faculty. Yet even when policies have been established, institutions have difficulty maintaining these set ratios. On the whole, state policymakers have been wary to intrude on institutional autonomy, and institutions have been unwilling to give in to this clause in collective bargaining.

Modify Tenure

Over the past twenty years, calls have been made to reexamine tenure and to replace the single profile or standard, which focuses mostly on research, to a broader profile or set of profiles that focus more on teaching or a balance of teaching, research, and service (Schell and Stock, 2001). Between those who wish to remove tenure completely and those who would like to maintain traditional tenure lies a middle ground: tenure restructured. In 1999, "52 percent of faculty surveyed (both tenured and nontenured) indicated that tenure should be modified but not altogether eliminated. And only 39 percent of tenured and 28 percent of nontenured thought tenure should remain as is" (Chait, 2005, p. 16). *Scholarship Reconsidered* (Boyer, 1990) is often used to center discussions about changing tenure standards. The critique that is always raised by these types of proposals is that it will create a bifurcated faculty, where those who are not primarily focused on research will become second-class citizens. This concern seems perhaps ironic when the professoriate has already turned into, at the very least, a two-class system of tenure-track and non-tenure-track faculty.

Some campuses have shifted their tenure standards, making it possible for individuals with a more exclusive portfolio of teaching to have the possibility for tenure. If more institutions had adopted such reforms earlier, we may not have had a tremendous growth in non-tenure-track faculty. The major growth has been in full-time non-tenure-track faculty with a focus on teaching. If the faculty as a profession is willing to fundamentally reform tenure standards, this process may be a way to achieve the conversion noted in the AAUP report. It is important to note, however, that the AAUP recommendations for teaching exclusively tenured positions conflict with deeply embedded assumptions at many research and doctoral campuses, where tenure is granted primarily based on research accomplishments. But many campuses have begun to move in this direction of rethinking tenure.

Eradicate Tenure and Move to All Long-Term Renewable Contracts

Some proposals have suggested eradicating tenure and following existing models of campuses that have never had tenure such as Evergreen State or have moved to eliminate tenure like Hampshire College (Chait and Trower 1997; Chait and Ford, 1982; Chait, 2005). Not-for-profit institutions without tenure tend to have long-term renewable contracts and intentional policies and practices in place for appropriate working conditions for all employees. Critics have noted that concerns about tenure are wide-ranging: from the abdication of undergraduate education and emphasis on teaching, the lack of flexibility to hire in new program areas and to reflect changes in fields, the financial strain on institutions, and the inability to provide regular feedback on performance (Chait and Ford, 1982). Studies of institutions without tenure suggest that faculty turnover is not as great as predicted, lack of tenure has no impact on morale or performance, faculty were just as satisfied at campuses without tenure, recruitment is not affected, and academic freedom can be provided (Chait and Ford, 1982).

Evidence suggests, however, that campuses with a tenure system have a greater faculty voice in governance and greater sway in institutional operations than institutions with contracts (Chait, 2005). The differences between the tenure and nontenure systems (a fully implemented contract system and a tenure one different from what we have today, as contract faculty are not part of any intentional system) appear relatively minor, however. A contract system ensures that the faculty is not bifurcated, as all faculty would have the same general working conditions. Additionally, the system is touted for having more flexibility because people can choose contract terms that best suit their lifestyles and interests. It may be easier with such a system to work thirty hours per week, leaving more time to care for children or dependents, for example. Chait (2005) suggests, however, that eradicating tenure internally is unlikely without external pressure, as the academy still generally supports a tenure system as the best professional career track. It should be noted that student outcomes have not been studied when comparing these two contract types. In a recent *New York Times* opinion piece, Trower (2010) suggested that the academic enterprise needs to go farther in thinking about faculty roles and contracts and suggested a summit to completely rethink both tenure-track and non-tenure-track positions, perhaps developing entirely new appointment types altogether such as long-term contracts.

Professionalize Non-Tenure-Track Faculty

The most touted recommendation is to professionalize non-tenure-track faculty by developing systematic multiyear contracts with greater equity in pay and benefits, creating intentional hiring and socialization processes, and including them in the institution's regular policies and programs, ranging from orientation to governance to evaluation (American Federation of Teachers, 2005; Baldwin and Chronister, 2001; Cross and Goldenberg, 2009; Gappa and Leslie, 1993). We discuss this recommendation in more detail in "Promising Practices and Policies" as this option is the direction most described in the literature. The concerns raised by those with other proposals (such as quotas for tenure or reforming tenure), however, indicate that professionalizing non-tenure-track faculty may fundamentally undermine the prospects of bringing back a tenured academy. In addition, this approach may not look at overall staffing patterns and come up with a desired profile of the faculty.

Create Hybrid Institutions

The choice between having some faculty on the tenure track and others not is typically made by the administration. Another option is to create colleges where faculty can opt for either contract. Chait and Trower (1997) note that some institutions give faculty a choice between tenure and a multiterm contract. Regardless of the choice, both tenure and non-tenure-track faculty are held to the same standards and criteria and are given benefits and equitable treatment. Some might wonder why anyone would choose a non-tenure-track path, but research demonstrates that some faculty want to focus on teaching and would choose this track if the working conditions were more aligned. Chait and Trower (1997) also found that some of the hybrid schools offered more incentives to be nontenured such as premium salaries, summer stipends, one year of severance pay, and sabbaticals. These incentives, paired with the possibility of less emphasis on research, were attractive to many faculty.

We recommend that policymakers and leaders start by addressing the broad direction. They should take time to first determine the desired staffing arrangements and then move toward that arrangement. If leaders believe the best route is to professionalize the non-tenure-track faculty, then we offer more details below. Certainly not all of these proposals are mutually exclusive (though some do not work together), and many can be combined, depending on the specific context. One might choose to work on tenure quotas, professionalize the non-tenure-track lines, and perhaps rethink the number and type of tenure-track and non-tenure-track lines. Perhaps the quota set for tenure track lines would include reformed tenure guidelines that allow for broader profiles for tenure. Maybe all non-tenure-track faculty will be part time and reserved for specialized fields. These types of changes would all be developed within a broader staffing plan for the campus. Without a broader direction or plan, institutions run the risk of again becoming reactionary to immediate concerns and influences without looking toward long-term investments, resulting in a repeat of the status quo.

Altbach (2000) reminds us that no worldwide norm exists for the faculty role. In China and Japan, for example, faculty are given permanent appointments at the time they are hired, regardless of rank. In Latin America, tenure as it is known in Europe and North America does not exist, and non-tenure-track faculty are the majority of teaching appointments there. In Europe, the situation varies from having many faculty on the tenure track (90 percent in Italy) to far fewer (closer to 50 percent in Finland). In Germany, "72 percent of the teaching staff are on limited term appointments, without professional rank and without permanent tenure. The majority hold full-time appointments" (Altbach, 2000, p. 24). The United Kingdom has dramatically changed its academic appointments; traditional tenure systems were abolished in the 1980s for new people entering the profession. Academics were given civil service status before the 1980s, but currently their appointments are with the universities, providing fewer legal entitlements. The Netherlands has undergone a similar transformation in its academic appointments, moving away from tenure. The notion of academic freedom is quite different in countries such as China, Croatia, and Indonesia, where faculty have to be concerned about speaking out freely. Countries around the world are struggling with academic staffing patterns for the future, but it appears that the U.S. model will likely continue to have a strong impact on the direction other countries take. The casual and less reflective nature of the current academic staffing system in the United States could be considered an ethical lapse, as other countries pattern their systems on our uncalculated and untested direction.

We now review the most often cited direction for moving forward—professionalizing the non-tenure-track faculty—in more detail.

Promising Practices and Policies for Professionalizing Non-Tenure-Track Faculty

Administrators and tenure-track faculty may not feel compelled by arguments about equity, inclusion, or ethical responsibility to change policies or practices to professionalize non-tenure-track faculty. The research on productivity, however, should be compelling to all parties on campus. Data suggests that the working conditions can affect productivity for all faculty (Bland and others, 2006). Bland and others (2006) list environmental characteristics that create productivity: thoughtful recruitment, clear mission and goals, shared culture of excellence, positive group climate, mentoring, communication and networks, resources, adequate work time, rewards, decentralized organization, and opportunities for professional development. Almost all of these departmental qualities are missing for non-tenure-track faculty. And not only non-tenure-track faculty are affected by the changes; tenure-track faculty would also be affected, as the features that characterize productive departments in the past will no longer be in operation for tenure-track faculty.

The major books and studies largely agree on the main actions needed to create equitable conditions for full-time and part-time non-tenure-track faculty (Cross and Goldenberg, 2009; Gappa and Leslie, 1993; Baldwin and Chronister, 2001; Gappa, Austin, and Trice, 2007; Hollenshead and others, 2007): communicating that non-tenure-track faculty are valued and respected; regularizing faculty hiring; systematizing the socialization process; establishing multiyear renewable contracts, seniority systems, guidelines for not rehiring individuals and revised reappointment procedures; offering fair compensation and benefits; defining faculty roles clearly; using promotion and evaluation systems; providing professional development; incorporating faculty into institutional governance; protecting academic freedom; and ensuring that faculty have the resources to meet their responsibilities. The recommendations do not differ markedly for part-time and full-time non-tenure-track faculty, but there are differences that should be attended to. Part-time faculty may not have the same type of promotion schedule or as much involvement in governance, for example.

Trower (2000), a comprehensive review of contract provisions and language beneficial for non-tenure-track faculty, is a good resource for administrators interested in professionalizing the non-tenure-track faculty. Much of contract language focuses on full-time non-tenure-track faculty, and the general trend is that the language is kept ambiguous to enable institutions to be flexible regarding full-timers' roles and responsibilities. For example, Shavers (2000) notes that only 12 of the 195 schools studied explicitly extend voting rights to full-time non-tenure-track faculty, and very few acknowledge time in rank. Rule (2000) found that non-tenure-track faculty are often included in academic freedom statements under all faculty.

Communicate a Message of Respect

This recommendation is often listed last in the various reports and books on non-tenure-track faculty, but we believe it is important to list it first because our own research suggests that campuses that institutionalize better policies and practices for non-tenure-track faculty started by communicating the message that non-tenure-track faculty are valued and respected (Kezar and Sam, 2010a). Gappa and Leslie (1993) and Kezar, Lester, and Anderson (2006) emphasize the importance of addressing negative messages and stereotypes.

as people often unconsciously develop a lack of respect for non-tenure-track faculty. Unless these perspectives are addressed, implementing any new policies or practices will be resisted. Gappa and Leslie (1993) note that associating quality with the number of tenure-track faculty in a program or department is one example of a negative message. Additionally, positive messages about non-tenure-track faculty should be made more explicit and public—in departmental meetings, awards ceremonies, and presidential speeches. Meaningful interaction between tenure-track faculty and non-tenure-track faculty is one of the best ways to increase this respect, so including non-tenure-track faculty in governance is extremely important in advancing the message that non-tenure-track faculty are valued members of the community.

Regularize Hiring

Cross and Goldenberg (2009) in particular demonstrate how non-tenure-track faculty are hired largely by departments without any standard procedures or processes. In fact, administrators generally have little understanding of the process used to hire non-tenure-track faculty. A more rigorous and standardized process of hiring should be developed that mirrors the current system of hiring tenure-track faculty. As Hollenshead and others (2007) note, the tendency is to put far more effort into hiring full-time than part-time non-tenure-track faculty, because the perception is that full-time faculty will be on campus for a much longer time. Furthermore, they need to be recruited and selected based on stated qualities and needs of the department or program, not based on happenstance criteria such as being available or knowing someone in the department (Baldwin and Chronister, 2001). But regularizing hiring is difficult in some institutions where academic disciplines have much authority over hiring, particularly at research universities or in disciplines such as physics. These disciplines and institutions may have little incentive to rethink hiring, and the administration may have very limited control over their hiring processes. Nevertheless, campus leadership should set the tone for hiring and staffing processes.

Create a Systematic Inclusion Process

Systems should be created to socialize non-tenure-track faculty, or non-tenure-track faculty should be included in current orientation and mentoring systems serving tenure-track faculty. A hallmark of professionals is that they socialize new members to the expectations and standards of the institution (Baldwin and Chronister, 2001; Gappa and Leslie, 1993; Sullivan, 2004). Non-tenure-track faculty need to be included in discussions about norms related to grading policies, teaching philosophy, cocurricular activities, and other campus processes. Tenure-track and senior non-tenure-track faculty who are familiar with the roles and responsibilities of the work should be included as mentors for non-tenure-track faculty. Often it is the practice to have other, more senior non-tenure-track faculty mentor newer non-tenure-track faculty. It is important to remove the barriers between the two groups so socialization can take place more easily, although for part-time faculty who are teaching in retirement and not interested in becoming part of the academic community, socialization may be less important. Again, motivation of the faculty is critical in developing meaningful policies and practices.

Rethink Hiring Practices

The current system of largely one-year contracts for full-time non-tenure-track faculty and semester-by-semester contracts for part-time faculty is not conducive to creating professionals who can invest meaningfully in the institution. The commitment of non-tenure-track faculty to their institutions is often a concern, though empirical evidence has shown otherwise; nevertheless, the perception is still prevalent. Commitment is a reciprocal endeavor. Perhaps institutions perceive a lack of commitment from non-tenure-track faculty because they lack commitment to non-tenure-track faculty. Most reports recommend that institutions offer multiyear renewable contracts, often starting with shorter contracts of two to three years and moving to five-year contracts after some probationary period of three to seven years (American Federation of Teachers, 2005; Baldwin and Chronister, 2001; Hollenshead and others 2007; Rhoades and Maitland, 2008). They also recommended that institutions eradicate policies that cap the number of years teaching off the tenure track.

For part-timers, creating a seniority system in which they receive priority appointments for teaching demonstrates the institution's commitment to them. Reports recommend that contract renewal and termination dates be explicitly listed and honored (Baldwin and Chronister, 2001). If multiyear contracts cannot be established, then some system of seniority can also be helpful. Once faculty have taught for a certain number of semesters, they might be eligible before other faculty for teaching assignments the next semester (a process used for part-time faculty at some institutions). For any type of contract, due process is recommended, whereby faculty are given some explanation for not being rehired, particularly those who have been long-term employees of the institution and demonstrated effective performance (Gappa and Leslie, 1993).

Offer Compensation and Benefits

Almost all reports call for equitable compensation and benefits, but often they do not provide details because compensation depends on whether a faculty member is full time or part time and varies with an institution's financial situation (Baldwin and Chronister, 2001; Gappa and Leslie, 1993; Hollenshead and others, 2007; Rhoades and Maitland, 2008). But all reports recommend—when feasible—that institutions provide more equitable pay and benefits, particularly for health care and retirement, or at least provide options. Many propose salary and benefits for full-time non-tenure-track faculty equal to those of entry-level tenure track faculty (American Federation of Teachers, 2005). For part timers in particular, office hours, governance, and service requirements need to be included in a discussion of salary (American Federation of Teachers, 2002). If part-timers are expected to hold office hours or participate in governance, they should be paid for this work. Moreover, scholars recommend consistent compensation across different departments in an institution. The common practice of paying non-tenure-track faculty different amounts in the same institution creates feelings of inequity (Gappa and Leslie, 1993).

Define Roles Clearly

Various scholars promote the need to better define the non-tenure-track faculty role, particularly for full-timers where expectations have been changing (Baldwin and Chronister, 2001; Hollenshead and others, 2007; Rhoades and Maitland, 2008). Issues such as office hours, class preparation, communicating with students, administrative responsibilities, supervising clinical or fieldwork, committee work, training, and mentoring graduate students all need to be made explicit in contracts or faculty handbooks. They should also be included in promotion and evaluation processes. Non-tenure-track faculty have experienced being assigned responsibilities and then given poor evaluations because the evaluations are not based on the role they had been assigned (Baldwin and Chronister, 2001). The expanding range of activities of full-time non-tenure-track faculty is reason for concern and necessitates greater and clearer definition of roles.

Use Promotion and Evaluation Systems

Non-tenure-track faculty are much more likely to feel like professionals if a system of sequential ranks and opportunities for salary increases is available (American Federation of Teachers, 2005; Baldwin and Chronister, 2001). Standards need to be developed for progression through the salary scale. To advance professionally, some suggest that a system of evaluation be put in place that is responsive to and aligned with their role, which is more focused on teaching (Gappa and Leslie, 1993). Gappa and Leslie (1993) also recommend that evaluation processes can be used as part of reappointment decisions.

The unions differ, however, and are leery about evaluations becoming part of the reappointment process. They argue that too often institutions rely on weak indicators such as student evaluations alone; therefore, there is less agreement about the desirability or use of evaluations. Reports recommend that non-tenure-track faculty be involved in the development of the promotion and the evaluation systems (Baldwin and Chronister, 2001). In addition, if peer evaluation processes are used, care should be taken that both tenure-track and non-tenure-track faculty are included.

Provide Opportunities for Professional Development

As articulated by O'Meara, Terosky, and Neumann (2008), one of the most important aspects of being a professional in academe is the ability to learn and grow over the course of one's career; this aspect is significantly related to being a productive and effective faculty member. Researchers recommend that non-tenure-track faculty be provided opportunities and support for professional development (Baldwin and Chronister, 2001; Gappa and Leslie, 1993). This recommendation includes issues ranging from funds for conferences to opportunities for professional growth, similar to sabbaticals. It is also important that centers for teaching and learning develop workshops and programs specifically designed for non-tenure-track faculty, so they have the opportunity to network on topics of specific interest to this population such as the scholarship of teaching.

It is also important, however, for campuses to offer professional development during which both groups have the opportunity to learn together—for example, programs on including collaborative learning or using technology. Non-tenure-track faculty should be included in awards and the recognition of teaching and service. One model effort (http://4faculty.org[7]) was created in California for serving the professional development needs of part-time faculty throughout the community college system. It is a cost-effective means of orientation and professional development across a host of institutions, covering topics that focus on the characteristics of community colleges and their students, building a syllabus, assessment, learning theories, and student support, including serving diverse students (Kauffman, 2005). Consortia across similar institutions may be an important direction for creating affordable professional development.

Incorporate Faculty in Institutional Governance

A long-held characteristic of professionals is their involvement in creating their conditions of work and affecting the larger work environment. As professionals, non-tenure-track faculty should be full participants in the governance process (American Federation of Teachers, 2005; Baldwin and Chronister, 2001; Rhoades and Maitland, 2008). Token representation and an invitation to participate are not sufficient; non-tenure-track faculty need to be given the right to an equal vote, to have a proportional number of members on committees and the faculty senate, and to be included in all matters, particularly curriculum, teaching, and learning, with the exception of tenure decisions. Involvement in governance should include the faculty senate, campuswide committees, and departmental decisions such as input in course selections and scheduling (Hollenshead and others, 2007). Moreover, non-tenure-track faculty should be paid or compensated for their involvement in governance.

Protect Academic Freedom

Baldwin and Chronister (2001) found that academic freedom as it relates to shared governance was more of a concern for full-time non-tenure-track faculty than academic freedom in the classroom. The results are similar for part-time faculty (American Federation of Teachers, 2010; Conley and Leslie, 2002). As a result, particular protections should be in place so that non-tenure-track faculty feel they can participate in governance without jeopardizing their jobs. Scholars recommended that campuses create explicit statements that protect individuals when they are critical of the administration as part of their shared governance role (Rhoades and Maitland, 2008). The move toward more multi-year contracts and an evaluation system could assist in this process as well.

Ensure Necessary Resources

Even in businesses, employers are supposed to provide the necessary supplies and support for employees to be able to fulfill their job responsibilities. This requirement should not be an exemption for academic institutions. Faculty need to be provided an office or shared office space that provides a place to meet with students and other colleagues, prepare for teaching, and meet other job responsibilities, from managing graduate assistance to field placements (Baldwin and Chronister, 2001; Gappa and Leslie, 1993). They also need appropriate clerical support for their teaching, service, and research demands and appropriate access to equipment such as a computer, photocopier, phone, facsimile machine, and other basic office equipment. Too often, non-tenure-track faculty, particularly part-timers, are expected to have a home office with all these materials and to buy their own supplies, putting an undue burden on faculty who are already paid less than their colleagues (Baldwin and Chronister, 2001; Gappa and Leslie, 1993).

Context-Based Examples of the Professionalization of Non-Tenure-Track Faculty

We assume that the professionalization of non-tenure-track faculty needs to be context based. In studies by Gappa and Leslie (1993) and Baldwin and Chronister (2001), the use of non-tenure-track faculty was based on the particular mission, past decisions and policies, a particular mix of programs, and the history of the institution. For each recommendation they make, they note that it must be modified to suit local conditions. Similarly, Schell and Stock (2001) call for more literature that documents meaningful reforms and changes that are context based and take into account differences among non-tenure-track faculty. They feel that too many ideas for improving working conditions for non-tenure-track faculty have been highly generalized and not examined the site-specific changes needed in programs, departments, colleges, and universities. One of our major assumptions about productive ways to move forward is that solutions need to take into account the institutional context and different typology of non-tenure-track faculty to provide solutions that better serve different groups in varying institutions. Thus, we join Baldwin and Chronister, Schell and Stock, and Gappa and Leslie in their calls for site-specific changes and innovations.

Gappa and Leslie (1993) and Schell and Stock (2001) call for more literature that documents meaningful context-based reforms that take into account differences among non-tenure-track faculty. This section reviews two different hypothetical institutions and their efforts to institutionalize change and demonstrates how these generalized principles need to be implemented quite differently. We highlight specific differences for part-time and full-time non-tenure-track faculty related to dilemmas and solutions. These cases draw on our review of the literature for working conditions and solutions.

Private Research University

One private research university has been considering ways to improve policies and practices for non-tenure-track faculty. Non-tenure-track faculty make up 50 percent of the total faculty, a large percentage of which are full time. It is hard to know exactly how many part-time faculty teach there, as the institution does not keep accurate records, but data suggest that many courses each term are also taught by part-time faculty. This institution needs to address full-time non-tenure-track faculty in particular, as their number has grown tremendously in recent years. Like most institutions, the university does not recognize the need to educate tenure-track faculty about the working conditions of non-tenure-track faculty or address negative messages, so non-tenure-track faculty experience outright backlash from tenure-track faculty at proposals for change. The climate at this university is very negative toward those not on the tenure track, and a clear two-tier system is in place.

Because the school's administration is very decentralized, enacting unilateral change is at first difficult. For example, creating uniform hiring practices proves challenging. Deans and department chairs have very individual approaches to hiring. The provost calls for schools to devise standards and criteria for hiring both full-time and part-time non-tenure-track faculty. Schools have to submit plans and report annually on their progress to develop and meet the new hiring procedures. Making the analogy to these already existing affirmative action plans helps schools to understand how they might approach this process. Schools in the university manage their own budgets so contract terms are decided locally, but the provost recommends a new plan of multi-year contracts with a promotion schedule. The plan provides that although salaries vary by school, all full-time faculty should receive generally similar pay (this factor has not been a major issue at the school, as the pay for full-time non-tenure-track faculty is on a par with that for tenure-track faculty). Because of the availability of part-time faculty who work in full-time jobs in other professions, pay for part-time faculty is at a lower range that fits the market situation of their discipline. Schools are encouraged to make part-time faculty who desire full-time work full time so that the issue of pay is alleviated. Several schools put this proposal into place immediately, but others are reluctant. To evaluate the progress over time, the provost provides money to the schools that made the changes, so data are available to report to the other schools to convince them of the value of such an approach. The provost organizes a campuswide orientation and invites non-tenure-track faculty for the first time. The orientation includes a breakout session for non-tenure-track faculty so they can also meet to discuss their specific needs. The number of full-time non-tenure-track faculty who attend is very high, but for part-time faculty is quite low. The administration recognizes that, because of part-time faculty's schedules, a one-time orientation may be less successful, so orientation for part-timers is available online to fit their schedules.

The faculty senate takes leadership for developing a subcommittee to look at professional development, governance, and mentoring of non-tenure-track faculty. This proposition requires some strong-arming from the administration, but luckily the provost finds a few allies among the faculty. The committee consists of non-tenure-track faculty across campus, so the role definition takes into account variations in the arts, medicine, law, and business. The committee recommends a formal mentoring program, which the provost funds, and the Center for Teaching and Learning begins to offer new seminars aimed at non-tenure-track faculty. The committee also develops a clear definition of the role for full-time non-tenure-track faculty, which the provost distributes to the deans. The faculty senate votes to include non-tenure-track faculty in all levels of governance. The senate asks for schools to report annually about the progress made regarding the inclusion of non-tenure-track faculty and using the new definition of the non-tenure-track role.

The subcommittee decides to conduct a survey of non-tenure-track faculty every other year to see how the mentoring, professional development, and governance are progressing and to explore changes in their working conditions. The first survey suggests that certain departments have much more severe problems with hostile climate than other departments. They have not changed their governance policies, even with the provost's mandate. The faculty senate realizes it will need to focus its efforts on certain schools that are not making progress. In addition, role definitions and suggested workloads for full-time non-tenure-track faculty are not being followed, and the workload for some greatly exceeds the faculty senate's recommendations.

The decentralized nature of the university means that constant surveying and reporting of all the schools is necessary and that faculty leaders need to apply pressure to schools that are not responding to administrative dictates for change. Non-tenure-track faculty in engineering and composition note feeling captive to tenured faculty, who define the rules of the game. The context-based solutions vary because of the decentralized administrative structure, strong faculty power, the focus on full-time over part-time non-tenure-track faculty, less of a need to address salary and benefits, more of a need to address access to resources (professional development) and professional levers (promotion scale and mentoring), and the overt hostility toward non-tenure-track faculty.

Community College

The situation is quite different for a community college that has no full-time non-tenure-track employees. Twenty-five percent of the faculty are tenured or tenure track, but 75 percent of the faculty are part-time, which has increased from 60 percent ten years ago. The campus climate is friendly between tenure-track and part-time faculty. Part-time faculty are recognized as making a major contribution to the campus. In this scenario, the administration is preventing change, believing that the part-time faculty are doing such a great job that they want to continue to use more of them. Without paying for benefits, the institution has more money for other costs, including a recently built student center. Tenured faculty's administrative and service loads have doubled in recent years. Some part-time faculty enjoy their positions, but more than half would prefer a full-time position and piece together classes at two or more colleges. Salary is quite low for part-timers, benefits are nonexistent, and seniority does not exist. The campus is in a state that cannot unionize, so collective bargaining is not an option. The campus actually has quite a few resources for part-time faculty, including a handbook, online and in-person orientation, access to governance and professional development related to teaching, and two professional development opportunities paid for each year.

Part-time faculty appeal to the tenured faculty for help, citing the dramatic decline in tenure-track positions and the increased workload for tenure-track faculty. The faculty senate decides to sit down with the administration with a proposal for changes to make working conditions more favorable for part-time faculty. The faculty develop an agenda of items for the administration to consider:

Request a plan looking at the right composition of full-time and part-time staff to run the campus adequately.

Convert some part-time positions into full-time tenure lines and move back toward 60 percent full-time teachers; note the literature and research about the problems of excessive numbers of part-time faculty on institutional operations and student outcomes.

Make part-timers eligible for benefits (prorated) and increase their pay over time to become closer to that of full-time faculty, making their use less attractive to the administration.

Create a seniority system so long-time part-timers have priority for teaching, and reward their commitment to the campus.

Include part-time faculty in the governance system more systematically and proportionally. Part-time faculty were added to the senate in recent years, but their voice is fairly invisible and they are not paid for involvement. The part-timers have convinced tenure-track faculty that it is in the best interests of them all for more part-timers on the senate.

Create policies around online courses, which are growing exponentially. Although part-timers teach most of them, full-timers are now being asked to teach them and recognize the problems of large class enrollments, workload, and intellectual property that need to be sorted out. Moreover, computer support and perhaps even replacement computers should be considered for those teaching extensively online.

Provide enough space for part-timers. One shared space for a part-timer is inadequate, given the rise in numbers and the need for more space.

Include office hours, course development, and service in the salary. Part-timers are currently not paid for many activities that they perform outside the classroom, making their pay even lower. Some part-time faculty cannot do this work without pay, and it is unethical to ask people to do work without any compensation.

The issues on this campus are quite different from the research university, which focused on full-time non-tenure-track faculty and the hostile culture among tenure-track faculty. At the community college, the faculty are united, but the administration has moved toward an inexpensive business model. The faculty have to work on key issues affecting working conditions, mostly compensation and resources.

The administration responds that given the high price tag for these issues, they need the list prioritized so they can address them over time. The faculty prioritize the list of items that require funding . . . suggesting that the administration look for other funding areas to divert to support some of these issues in the short term. Several faculty approach the local media about the concerns they have, and a story is run about the community college's dilemma and the rise in part-time faculty on campus. This event puts pressure on the administration to change some issues. In addition, the faculty have improved governance in recent years and have strong leadership in the senate to negotiate with the administration. Although the administration is taken aback at first, it later comes back with some proposals for diverting expenses from one area to pay for the part-time salary increase. They begin the road to change. Change will take a while on this campus, as the funding structure cannot support many of the changes immediately. The context of interest in this case is the largely part-time faculty, the diminished power of tenure-track faculty, the power of the administration, and the working conditions (largely framed around money rather than climate).

How Do We Accomplish These Changes and Ensure Intentionality?

For more than twenty-five years, detailed strategies and advice for creating more intentional approaches to the deployment of non-tenure-track faculty have existed, starting with Leslie, Kellams, and Gunne (1982), Gappa and Leslie (1993), and Baldwin and Chronister (2001). Professional groups such as the AAUP, the NEA, and the AFT have established standards of practice for non-tenure-track faculty (American Association of University Professsors, 2009; National Education Association, 2002; American Federation of Teachers, 2002). Repeatedly, ideas for creating greater equity, more intentional approaches to institutional operations, and fair employment policies and practices have been offered to guide administrators and the academy. Yet little progress has been made in changing institutional practice. Based on Slaughter and Rhoades's concept of academic capitalism (2004), the lack of progress can be tied to administrators' continuing to support corporate interests for revenue generation and market values over educational values, even though doing so clearly affects staffing and institutions negatively. Cross and Goldenberg (2009) suggest alternatively that little progress has been made because decision making for hiring in many institutions is decentralized and uncoordinated; thus, a unified campus movement is difficult to execute. Kezar and Sam (2009) conducted a national study looking at union contracts and campuses with model policies and practices in place for non-tenure-track faculty. Fewer than one hundred campuses could be identified as having made substantial progress, and only a handful have institutionalized positive policies and practices for non-tenure-track faculty. The slow progress suggests that perhaps more radical actions need to occur to create change in institutions, whether advocacy, collective bargaining, or some other form of activism.

Internal change based on implementation of appropriate practices has not penetrated the consciousness of higher education administrators, primarily chairs and deans. As noted through analysis of institutions that have better policies and practices in place for non-tenure-track faculty, unions have made the major progress in improving the working conditions for non-tenure-track faculty. And on campuses that have individually moved forward that were not unionized, non-tenure-track faculty themselves have led the charge for their improved working conditions (Kezar and Sam, 2010a), which suggests that change from the bottom up has been more successful and that although administrators have entertained ideas for change for twenty years, they do not appear invested or committed to creating better conditions for non-tenure-track faculty.

The proposals presented in most books and reports (aside from those created by the unions) offer plans and agendas for administrators to execute change. We review these proposals followed by change initiatives described from the bottom up. As noted above, we are concerned there appears no motivation among those in positions of authority to implement plans, as they have been slow to act for many years already. Furthermore, we realize that change must not only be the responsibility of those from the top but also those from the bottom up.

Professionalizing from the Top Down

We are hopeful that administrators will take up our challenge to deliberate and be thoughtful about the makeup of their faculty. The following are recommendations for making non-tenure-track faculty more purposively part of the faculty and creating a more systematic career.

Develop an academic staffing plan. Although most scholars do not recommend a specific numeric proportion of tenure-track to non-tenure-track faculty, most agree that campuses need to develop an academic staffing plan that determines their goals for the use of non-tenure-track faculty based on the educational mission. They also need to determine what the appropriate ratio is of tenure-track to non-tenure-track faculty, full time and part time, and in what areas these faculty should be deployed (Baldwin and Chronister, 2001; Gappa and Leslie, 1993). To develop an academic staffing plan, scholars recommend an audit of academic personnel, examining what information is currently collected and what needed information is missing. Although hiring might happen locally, similar to that for tenure-track faculty, hiring processes may need vetting through more senior levels to ensure that agreed-upon plans are being followed and that the philosophy articulated in the plan is enacted in particular departments (Gappa and Leslie, 1993). There must be accountability for the generated academic staffing plan, and the staffing plan must be reviewed and reevaluated as conditions and times change.

Monitor the use of non-tenure-track faculty and understand their experiences. To understand whether the academic plan is being implemented campuswide, more data must be collected, particularly about the non-tenure-track faculty's perceptions of change on campus (Chait and Ford, 1982; Gappa and Leslie, 1993). Faculty databases should be able to identify the non-tenure-track faculty, contract details, their progression and promotion, and other information. Having databases allows for problems to be identified such as departments where non-tenure-track faculty are not being promoted or inequities in pay. Details about databases are offered in both Chait and Ford (1982) and Gappa and Leslie (1993). In addition to ongoing information related to contracts, it is important to occasionally conduct surveys of the non-tenure-track faculty to see how new policies and practices are being implemented and what needs to be changed. During the first five years of implementation, annual collection of data might be helpful.

Create a campuswide representative body to provide advice on staffing. As Gappa and Leslie (1993) note, "A standing forum ensures that issues that might otherwise be left unsaid and unheard will be brought up into the open" (p. 247). A standing committee should be created that is dedicated to improving the working conditions for non-tenure-track faculty, providing a place and space for faculty to brainstorm ideas and express concerns from across campus. These insights and concerns can inform staffing plans in the development of policies and procedures. In a recent study of campuses implementing improved policies and procedures for non-tenure-track faculty, the creation of a campuswide committee or steering group was critical to implementing change, particularly at nonunion campuses (Kezar and Sam, 2009). The committee is also a way to make systemic, rather than piecemeal, change. For example, a campus might develop a new evaluation system but not socialize any faculty to the system. The committee would look at practice and policy changes as a whole and link needed changes in evaluation to socialization, professional development, and orientation. Data collected on campus can be reviewed by the committee and used to recommend ongoing changes to policies and practices.

Include multiple stakeholders in the change process and target key groups. All players must be part of efforts to professionalize non-tenure-track faculty, including non-tenure-track faculty, deans and department chairs, faculty assemblies, senior administrative leaders, unions and professional associations such as the AAUP, and governing boards. Unless all these stakeholders are aware of the reasons for changing the working conditions for non-tenure-track faculty and are familiarized with the proposed changes, uneven implementation and resistance to change are likely. A variety of different studies have demonstrated that department chairs (and sometimes deans) have the most impact on the hiring and general policies related to non-tenure-track faculty (Cross and Goldenberg, 2009; Gappa and Leslie, 1993). As a result, any plans moving forward should integrate department chairs and deans. Many campuses have begun training for department chairs, which would be an excellent venue for indicating institutional goals and objectives related to non-tenure-track faculty. At present, most training focuses on recruiting and hiring tenure-track faculty and sometimes faculty diversity. The topic of non-tenure-track faculty is rarely addressed, but if it is, the institution does not have a thoughtful plan or set of policies that it communicates to chairs.

Professionalizing from the Bottom Up

Proposals to professionalize non-tenure-track faculty are often aimed at administrators who have authority to organize the various stakeholders. Unfortunately, administrators who are best positioned to institute the changes have not met this challenge. Therefore, we offer recommendations for including multiple stakeholders aimed at non-tenure-track faculty leaders creating change from the bottom up. Studies conducted of the non-tenure-track faculty's leading efforts to change policies and practices note that they work with non-tenure-track faculty organizations such as the Coalition of Contingent Academic Labor (COCAL), students, the media, and unions. These organizations are often interested in communicating their concerns about the working conditions of non-tenure-track faculty and the need for change (Schell and Stock, 2001). Over the last fifteen years, various grassroots coalitions have formed to provide a voice for non-tenure-track faculty; they can be sources of support for bottom-up change. For example, The Adjunct Nation produced a series of publications such as *The Adjunct Advocate* aimed at helping non-tenure-track faculty deal with the difficult working conditions they often encounter. The same organization also creates publications for administrators to understand how to create better working conditions for adjunct faculty. In more recent years, a new organization, New Faculty Majority (NFM—see http://www.newfacultymajority.info/national/) is aimed at uniting non-tenure-track faculty across a variety of groups. Traditionally, different organizations represented part-time and full-time non-tenure-track faculty separately. The New Faculty Majority aims to create a unified front across all the differences that may have prevented collective action.

Union processes for creating change are already well documented in many resources; see the NEA, AFT, and AAUP Web sites for information about union organizing and some publications (American Federation of Teachers, 2005; Rhoades, 1998, 1996). This section documents changes by non-tenure-track faculty that occurred outside unions (as many states do not allow union organizing) so that other bottom-up approaches to change can be better understood. These changes are based largely on a recent study by Kezar and Sam (2009). Non-tenure-track faculty leaders rely on some of the strategies of top-down leaders such as gathering data or creating a campuswide committee. Yet they also display certain distinctive strategies. In addition, national groups and partnerships typically aid local efforts. For example, the COCAL and the NFM provide national networks to help facilitate change on individual campuses. They also seek legislative and broader policy changes that would support local changes.

Mobilize. For change to begin from the bottom up, non-tenure-track faculty need to mobilize. Mobilization is unlikely to occur, however, unless faculty create awareness and overcome apathy among their peers, including other non-tenure-track faculty. They can create awareness by spreading information about a galvanizing event (such as a person's being unfairly fired), collecting data about salaries and benefits compared with tenure-track faculty, demonstrating poor working conditions, or sharing research about poor working conditions. Mobilizing is also enhanced when non-tenure-track faculty become more visible on campus, which helps develop allies among other groups on campus. A powerful mechanism for breaking invisibility is to distribute data, making other people aware of the sheer number of non-tenure-track faculty on campus and their extremely low pay.

Create a plan of action. Non-tenure-track faculty were more successful in their efforts when they had an action plan, similar to the staffing plan of the top-down approach. So that change is systemic, it is important that non-tenure-track faculty leaders think about a broad vision for change on campus that includes all the areas we listed under best practices and policies and works over time. Having a plan provides a blueprint for actions as part of governance, what data to collect, what allies to target, and what external sources of support are available. The community college example listed above provided an agenda that became a plan of action once it was prioritized.

Use data, benchmarks, and models. Non-tenure-track faculty leaders, similar to union leaders, use data to mobilize people and make them aware of inequitable pay and benefits. As they move to alter campus policies and practices, campuses identified some model campuses through listservs or from calling peer campuses, which had seniority or benefits policy they wanted to mirror. Leaders were careful to identify models and benchmarks of institutions similar to their type of campus. They used the data to develop an action plan for implementing changes. Unlike administrators, however, faculty leaders are often not allowed access to data. In fact, many administrators specifically refuse to share data, because it would empower non-tenure-track faculty. Data can be obtained about institutions, however. The AFT has created an online tool that allows a person to search specific institutions and find reports on salary and faculty and to compare with other schools in the area (see http://highereddata.aft.org).

Create a regular meeting task force or committee. Creating regular meetings of non-tenure-track faculty (and often including tenure-track faculty) through a task force or committee charged with investigating non-tenure-track faculty work conditions is important for implementation. At various campuses, such committees were often established through the faculty senate. Rather than a committee created by the administration, the faculty formed these committees themselves.

Participate in governance. One of the most important ways for non-tenure-track faculty to make a significant difference in broad policies and practices is to gain access and play a leadership role in the governance process. Campuses that have made major progress usually have a non-tenure-track faculty member who has played a leadership role on the academic senate and recommended new practices such as making professional development available. Several non-tenure-track leaders pronounced that governance was the most important factor to implementing and institutionalizing change. One challenge to participation in governance is to create a system that encourages participation through compensation for involvement or some other form of incentive rather than making participation a burden.

Garner outside pressure. Some campuses progressed to a certain point and then stalled, for example, obtaining only minor salary increases and marginal health benefits that they have to pay for and then being unable to move forward. Others mobilized but were mired in long-term discussions about policies or could not get the institution to engage in discussions. In these many instances, garnering outside pressure from unions, media, students, parents, and accreditors was a way to push forward the implementation. The community college discussed earlier used the media to apply pressure.

Identify allies. In terms of advocacy for changing the working conditions of non-tenure-track faculty, administrators reported that non-tenure-track faculty themselves were the most significant advocates, followed by executive administrators, department chairs, and the faculty senate (Hollenshead and others, 2007). Yet in a question about those who resisted change most on campus, executive administrators and tenure-track faculty were listed most often, followed by department chairs. Thus, non-tenure-track faculty should actively seek out potential allies from different groups, but be aware that no group is automatically considered one.

Use allies. For policies to be successful, they must translate down to departments, but often policies are not uniformly enforced throughout the campus. One approach is pressing administrators to hold departments accountable. Another way to overcome this challenge is to use allies in departments to leverage changes. By creating five or six model departments on campus with good policies and practices, it becomes harder for other departments to ignore the issue. Tenure-track faculty will start to discuss the problems of non-tenure-track faculty at senate meetings more vociferously, pressuring departments that did not follow the policy.

Address climate. Campuses often have policies and practices in place that exclude non-tenure-track faculty, but no one has examined them. To address the climate, non-tenure-track faculty should scan campus practices for inequalities: invitations to events, access to funding and resources, evaluation and assessment, curriculum development, administrative support, leadership opportunities, and the like. One critical aspect for addressing the climate and inequitable policies and practices is being able to discuss sensitive issues in senate meetings such as the growth of non-tenure-track faculty as a challenge to the institution of tenure, the importance of protecting tenure-track and full-time jobs while also obtaining parity for non-tenure-track faculty, whether absolute parity in pay or benefits is the final outcome of change, and viewing non-tenure-track faculty as good teachers but realizing that their working conditions affect quality. If such issues are not discussed openly, they can create tension and block change.

Conclusion

Many proposals and recommendations have been offered for addressing the change in the composition of the faculty, yet no clear path exists. This chapter presented macrocourses of action to be considered for developing a path forward for reconfiguring the nature of labor in the academy and provided more detail on the direction that has had the most agreement about professionalizing the non-tenure-track faculty. It offered examples from a private research university and community college about possible ways to professionalize the faculty. Last, it reviewed strategies for moving forward in rethinking the work lives of non-tenure-track faculty from the top down and the bottom up.

The goal of this monograph is to review the many proposals and action plans for professionalizing non-tenure-track faculty, not to offer a specific plan to do so. We believe it is important to provide all perspectives, as one of the issues limiting progress forward may be ideological tensions. We hope that by acknowledging these perspectives and bringing them together, we can foster more dialogue toward an amiable solution. We also hope that by pairing the plans of action with our known data and research a better platform for moving forward can be based on facts rather than biases and misconceptions.

Conclusions for Practice and Suggestions for Further Research

> If we want things to stay as they are, things will have to change.
>
> —Giuseppe di Lampedusa, cited in Hamilton
> and Gaff, 2009, p. 19

IF THE ACADEMY WANTS TO RETAIN IMPORTANT ASPECTS from the past, it will need to change dramatically in the future. Paradoxically, change may be what is needed to preserve some of the key historical features of the academy that are still important, even in this global world and changing economy. This need for change and the complexities of this process are captured in Anson and Jewell (2001), which reflects a dialogue between a tenured faculty member (Anson) and a nontenured faculty member (Jewell) as they sort out the changes in the academy through their own stories. Jewell recounts his experiences—the lack of rights often associated with a non-tenure-track line, the fear and anxiety about reemployment, and the overall disenfranchisement and exploitation as a non-tenure-track faculty member. Anson speaks of his experiences as director of the writing program, administrative pressures to hire non-tenure-track faculty, and the ethical issues that surrounded his choices. The results are a tangle of interconnected experiences, motivations, concerns, and ethical dilemmas and the vexing situation the academy finds itself in. Both Anson and Jewell look for large reform to happen in the academy but are unsure that the academy alone can change as necessary.

This chapter addresses the challenges that Jewell and Anson struggle with and offers a set of conclusions organized around the reviews of research (see "Portrait of Non-Tenure-Track Faculty" and "Experiences of Non-Tenure-Track

Faculty") and of recommendations for policy and practice. The recommen- dations for policy and practice advanced in this chapter emanate from a syn thesis of the implications presented in the previous chapters of thi monograph. Suggestions for further research help to provide a direction fo change as it relates to research. We need vastly different research to guide u toward better solutions.

Overall Conclusions and Implications

Limited knowledge: Our synthesis of the literature suggests that we sorely neec more research about non-tenure-track faculty. Important differences ir part-time versus full-time work, motivation, and department, discipline and institutional type have not been examined, making most generaliza tions inaccurate for a large number of non-tenure-track faculty. We know most about differences between part-time and full-time non-tenure-tracl faculty but lack knowledge of other key differences that shape experience and would help create more fine-grained policy.

Non-tenure-track faculty as hybrids: Studies demonstrate the commitment intrinsic motivation, and involvement of non-tenure-track faculty, man) of whom view themselves as professionals who have in-depth training anc have been socialized to the norms of the academy. Action plans createc by those who work most closely with non-tenure-track faculty, including the unions, treat non-tenure-track faculty as professionals. Yet studies alsc demonstrate that the working conditions of some non-tenure-track fac- ulty position them as laborers rather than professionals. It seems that wc can advance the issue best by treating them as hybrids, both profession- als and employees.

Non-tenure-track faculty as heterogeneous: Department, school, campus, anc state policy will benefit from understanding that no single "typical" non- tenure-track faculty member exists but that working conditions vary widel) between part-timers and full-timers. In addition, leaders need to under- stand the other major differences: age, education, motivation, discipline time with the institution, department, and institutional type. Thesc differences are related to, among others, needs, concerns, contributions experiences, satisfaction, and commitment of non-tenure-track faculty. These differences need to be acknowledged and explored in the collection of data to create campus policy.

Union: Collective bargaining has been demonstrated to improve the working conditions for non-tenure-track faculty. It appears that unionization is a proven strategy for professionalizing non-tenure-track faculty on campuses. This strategy may be successful because unions provide an organized and systematic way for change to occur from the bottom up. Unions also provide a sense of safety found in numbers that lone pockets of change may not have. A tension needs to be resolved in the academy. Professionals tend not to see the value in unionizing, and unions are suspicious of people who characterize themselves as professionals. Hollenshead and others' study (2007) of full-time non-tenure-track faculty found that almost none of them planned to unionize, even with poor working conditions. Yet, unions have not always been open to representing non-tenure-track faculty and on some campuses this may not be on appropriate avenue for change. Non-tenure-track faculty, with their hybrid identity, may be positioned to resolve the tension between professionalization and unionization. Yet to date it remains a problematic issue for moving forward with action plans—specifically, greater unionization.

Need for change: The existing data about the experiences and working conditions about non-tenure-track faculty clearly document the need for changes in policies and practices at most campuses. As Hollenshead and others (2007) so aptly note, although we may not meet the needs and concerns of all non-tenure-track faculty, we know that certain changes to professionalize the faculty will help some: longer-term contracts, equitable pay, better benefits, professional development, and the like. Even those non-tenure-track faculty who have no desire for change would not be adversely affected by these changes. Their suggestion for ongoing assessment of needs, as the non-tenure-track faculty workforce is provided new policies and practices, is important to remember. Ongoing institutional research is likely necessary until changes are fully implemented.

Academic staffing: In whichever direction they move, campuses should examine their entire academic staffing—part-time non-tenure-track, full-time non-tenure-track, and tenure-track faculty—to determine the appropriate staffing arrangement given the institution's mission and structure Most research suggests that decisions about academic staffing vary widely by institutional type and culture and should be made by individual institutions. State policies that try to mandate particular staffing arrangements may not be in the best interests of students, postsecondary institutions and non-tenure-track faculty.

Context-based changes: Two examples given earlier, the research university and the community college, demonstrate that plans of action and recommendations for moving forward need to be based on the institutional type and culture. Although global plans and ideas for professionalizing non-tenure-track faculty have been extremely helpful, they also have masked important variations that leaders should take into consideration as they institutionalize change. We need more case study research and examples of institutions that have altered their policies and practices to inform other institutions.

Professionalization: Different scholars and practitioners as well as non-tenure-track faculty themselves appear to broadly support professionalizing the non-tenure-track faculty above other plans of action and recommendations. See "Plans of Action and Promising Policies" for all of the practices that can be put in place to professionalize non-tenure-track faculty.

Support: Research demonstrates that non-tenure-track faculty themselves are responsible for the majority of changes on college campuses. They need more allies to create changes across the country; we recommend that tenure-track faculty join forces with non-tenure-track faculty and support their efforts as much as possible. On campuses with a supportive administration, we hope they provide non-tenure-track faculty with opportunities for leadership on campus. In addition to supporting non-tenure-track faculty on campuses, faculty and administrators can show their support by assisting national organizations such as the New Faculty Majority, the Coalition of Contingent Academic Labor, and unions on campus. Tenure-track faculty should recognize that as better salary and benefits are obtained for non-tenure-track faculty, continued proliferation is less likely

State policymakers: Although research suggests that strict regulations for addressing non-tenure-track faculty's issues might hamper certain campuses with distinctive cultures and institutional structures, it does not mean that state policy is not important for helping to create change for non-tenure-track faculty. Reports help to create awareness about the non-tenure-track faculty's issues, support campuses conducting their own research, and help to make changes in policies and practices.

Evaluation and data collection: A synthesis of the various studies makes it clear that changes are happening constantly and that ongoing research is needed to understand whether we are reaching the appropriate staffing arrangements on college campuses. We anticipate that more campuses will begin to use multiyear renewable contracts. To understand changes in the use of policy as well as new policies and new problems that emerge, we will need ongoing research. One emerging challenge is the expansion of the non-tenure-track faculty's role; what began primarily as a teaching role has now changed dramatically. As campuses try to address different concerns of non-tenure-track faculty, they will better succeed if they obtain ongoing input from non-tenure-track faculty. Evaluations should include input from all types of faculty, staff, and administration. The data collected would be better used if institutions made such data available to all stakeholders of the college or university; transparency is key.

Titles: The terminology used to describe non-tenure-track faculty is extremely important, and we need to come to some consensus about desirable terms. Returning to the general term "faculty" is perhaps the most desirable approach over the long term. We call on national groups and individual campuses to spend time discussing titles and developing a terminology that is respectful, meaningful, and informative in the short term.

Over- and underrepresentation: Racial minorities are underrepresented among part-time faculty, which may be an issue for campuses to investigate. Women tend to be overrepresented among both full-time and part-time non-tenure-track faculty. Gappa and Leslie (1993) found that affirmative action was not applied to these positions, which likely continues to be true. Campuses should examine the profile of their non-tenure-track faculty for inequities. But finding inequities does not necessarily mean a problem exists, as retired or older individuals are overrepresented among part-time faculty. Until this phenomenon is studied, however, we will not know whether it is an issue inherent in the current system.

Qualifications: The research demonstrates that hiring procedures are inadequate, requirements are often unclear, and standards are not established or held. Once hired, non-tenure-track faculty find their jobs constantly changing and may not meet the initial qualifications and expectations of the faculty member or the institution. Institutions need to think more carefully through their hiring process and come up with long-term strategies.

Research on the positive qualities of non-tenure-track faculty's work: Very few studies investigate the more positive qualities of non-tenure-track faculty careers. Although the focus on problems has perhaps more policy and practice recommendations, we can improve campus climate when we know what works well for non-tenure-track faculty. For example, studies might identify career paths and options for non-tenure-track faculty. And a focus on campuses that have improved and the promising policies and practices they have implemented can be helpful. Documenting inclusive non-tenure-track cultures provides role models for other institutions.

Future Research

Given that one of our observations is the inadequate knowledge we have about non-tenure-track faculty, it is not surprising that we have a list of future research areas: (1) the need for reliable national and state data, (2) studies that reflect the voice of non-tenure-track faculty, (3) studies based on context, and (4) studies that examine differences in motivation, discipline, department, and institutional type. Further recommendations for improving research are offered in Kezar and Sam (2010b).

Reliable and Ongoing National and State Data
Schuster and Finkelstein (2006) provided one of the best overall portraits of non-tenure-track faculty using NSOPF data (which is no longer available).

This landscape is ever changing, and it is important that we have data that examine and categorize non-tenure-track faculty. The number of full-time non-tenure-track faculty is increasing and the number of part-timers growing; it is important that we conduct more research to understand the current portrait of non-tenure-track faculty more accurately.

Several steps could be taken to improve the data available to understand non-tenure-track faculty. First, institutions need to establish more robust systems internally to track non-tenure-track faculty, particularly differences by contract and disciplines. Second, a systematic national dataset needs to be developed on all types of faculty. Perhaps UCLA's HERI faculty survey could focus more specifically on issues important to non-tenure-track faculty and explore differences in motivation, discipline, and institutional type. The recent changes to the survey are helpful, but we cannot leave the burden for this data collection on this center alone. It is important that a national database of faculty be reestablished to help inform policy, especially if states begin to create policies related to non-tenure-track faculty.

Third, it is important to note the significance of institutional and individual participation in such data collection. To better understand the trends that are occurring in higher education, whether through national or local studies, it is imperative for institutions and individuals to participate and ensure that their voices are heard. Incentives need to be created to obtain data from non-tenure-track faculty, particularly part-timers, who have not been prone to fill out phone or mail surveys.

A Voice for Non-Tenure-Track Faculty

One of the major deficits identified in empirical research is that we have little research studying the experiences and voices of non-tenure-track faculty themselves. A national database that surveys non-tenure-track faculty is no longer available. One recent national study conducted on non-tenure-track faculty examines administrators' perspective but did not survey non-tenure-track faculty themselves. Although we understand the working conditions of non-tenure-track faculty, we do not understand how they affect the lives of non-tenure-track faculty and how they vary among this heterogeneous group. We also understand very little about how the hostile climate on many campuses or the two-tier system affects their ability to successfully accomplish their roles. And we know very little about the psychological states of non-tenure-track faculty.

An emerging trend is for campus offices and services to survey non-tenure-track versus tenure-track faculty to determine the needs of each group so the campus can best support all faculty. Although one study compared the needs of non-tenure-track and tenure-track faculty for library use and found that they were largely the same, the situation may differ in other important areas (Wisneski, 2005). It remains an important direction for future research examining technology needs, fitness and wellness, and other support services.

Context-Based Studies

Although researchers conducting qualitative research and case studies acknowledge that institutional culture and structure affect the experiences of non-tenure-track faculty and appropriate policies and practices, most recommendations have been context free, deriving generalizations out of cases. We need more research that documents context-based solutions to address the concerns and issues of non-tenure-track faculty and studies that are formulated and framed with context as an important factor. Campus stories of change are an example of the type of context-based studies we need in the future. For example, O'Meara Terosky, and Neumann (2008) posit that the number of non-tenure-track faculty on a campus and how long they have been there might affect their satisfaction and the perception on campus.

Differences by Motivation, Department, Discipline, and Institutional Type

Perhaps the areas most in need of research are differences by motivation department, discipline, and institutional type. The few studies that examined motivations have found significant differences in the experiences, satisfaction and attitude of non-tenure-track faculty. But we know less about the impact of motivation because of the limited number of studies and research that look at differences in the non-tenure-track group. Earlier researchers developed typologies of non-tenure-track faculty that encompassed motivation and background, but little research has been done using these typologies to examine differences in the experiences, outcomes, and commitment of non-tenure-track faculty. Shaker (2008) also found a set of individual differences that need to be explored in more depth—age, educational degree, career path, and time at the institution. These elements made a significant difference in faculty's experiences and attitudes.

Discipline and institutional type have been investigated even less than motivation. Shaker's study (2008) is one of the few to examine a discipline—composition—in greater depth; some distinct perspectives resulted. For example, composition faculty tend to identify with their department more than the English discipline or the institution. They were cut off from tenure-track faculty and had little interaction with them. We suspect many other differences exist, for example, that salary, recruitment, hiring, and orientation differ by discipline and department. Future studies may want to further investigate this issue. Although institutional differences have not been examined in relation to satisfaction, the difference in working conditions at some institutions might also suggest some differences in satisfaction by institutional type that need to be researched in the future.

Conclusion

In the end, much work needs to be done to understand the dynamic landscape of non-tenure-track faculty. In the meantime, however, we hope to have accomplished five goals in this monograph: (1) to synthesize and analyze the research that is available on non-tenure-track faculty and thus give the reader a better understanding of these individuals as a heterogeneous group and their impact on higher education; (2) to offer different ways of conceptualizing and thinking about non-tenure-track faculty; (3) to offer some recommendations and plans of action so that campuses can move forward and policymakers can make important decisions to improve the working conditions of non-tenure-track faculty; and (4) to help lay down the foundation for reasoned, intelligent, and ethical dialogue among stakeholders by presenting data that can be used to address changes in the academy. Change is inevitable, and the current status quo cannot hold. "The academy can move with them, behind them, or ahead of them. The academy cannot, however, stand still" (Schell and Stock, 2001, p. 45). Paths forward look quite different, and we hope that the process comprises research, principled thought, and evidence-based decisions.

Notes

1. We use the term *non-tenure-track faculty* because it is one of the most recognized labels for this growing class of faculty. The monograph explains, however, how campuses use a variety of different terms. We also explore the idea of using the new terminology because the term *non-tenure-track* does not recognize the professional status that we argue for in the monograph.

2. Part-time faculty with tenure are not the norm compared with the appointments of the other 95 percent of part-time faculty who do not have tenure; thus, our use of the term "part-time faculty" focuses more on those members who are neither tenured nor on the tenure track.

3. Schuster and Finkelstein (2006) grouped fine arts, natural sciences, and social sciences together as the liberal arts, keeping the humanities as a separate category.

4. It is important to note, however, that some institutions such as the California State University System and the University of Michigan have established titles to indicate differences in experience, rank, and seniority to make up for this oversight. For example at the University of Michigan, Dearborn, full-time and part-time non-tenure-track faculty are Lecturers 1 to 4, with each level indicating seniority.

5. The numbers in this section are from faculty employed at the time in 1998 and do not necessarily include all faculty from previous years.

6. Schuster and Finkelstein (2006) found that 35 percent to be predominantly retirees from full-time positions and faculty who held full-time positions at one campus but were moonlighting at another for part-time work.

7. This website is currently still available for free use, but new content is no longer updated.

References

AFT Higher Education. (2005). *Standards of good practice in the employment of full-time non-tenure-track faculty: Professionals and colleagues.* Washington, DC: American Federation of Teachers.

Altbach, P. (2000). The deterioration of the academic estate: International patterns of academic work. In P. Altbach (Ed.), *The changing academic workplace: Comparative Perspectives* (pp. 1–33). Boston: Boston College Center for International Higher Education.

American Association of University Professors (AAUP). (2005). *Inequities persist for women and non-tenure-track faculty: The annual report on the economic status of the profession, 2004–2005.* Washington, DC: American Association of University Professors.

American Association of University Professors (AAUP). (2006). *Trends in faculty status, 1975–2003.* Retrieved March 6, 2010, from http://www.aaup.org/aaup/pubres/research/trends1975-2003.htm.

American Association of University Professors (AAUP). (2009). *Conversion of appointments to tenure track.* Retrieved, June 1, 2010, from http://www.aaup.org/AAUP/comm/rep/conversion.htm.

American Council on Education (ACE). (1981). *A recent survey on tenure practices.* Washington, DC: American Council on Education.

American Federation of Teachers. (2002). *Fairness and Equity: Standards of good practice in the employment of part-time adjunct faculty.* Washington DC: American Federation of Teachers.

American Federation of Teachers. (2003). *Full-time non-tenure-track faculty report.* Washington, DC: American Federation of Teachers.

American Federation of Teachers. (2005). *Reversing the course: The troubled state of academic staffing and the path forward.* Washington, DC: American Federation of Teachers.

American Federation of Teachers. (2009). *American academic: The state of higher education workforce, 1997–2007.* Washington, DC: American Federation of Teachers.

American Federation of Teachers. (2010). *American academic: A national survey of part-time/adjunct faculty.* Washington, DC: American Federation of Teachers.

Anderson, E. L. (2002). *The new professoriate: Characteristics, contributions, and compensation.* Washington, DC: American Council on Education.

Anson, C., and Jewell, R. (2001). Shadows of the mountain. In E. Schell and P. Stock (Eds.), *Moving a mountain: Transforming the role of non-tenure-track faculty in composition studies and higher education.* Urbana, IL: National Council of Teachers of English.

Antony, J. S., and Valdez, J. R. (2002). Exploring the satisfaction of part-time college faculty in the United States. *The Review of Higher Education, 26*(1), 41–56.

Arnold, J., Cooper, C. L., and Robertson, I. T. (1995). *Work psychology: Understanding human behaviour in the workplace.* London, UK: Pitman Publishing.

Association of American Universities (AAU). (2001). *Non-tenure-track faculty report.* Washington, DC: Association of American Universities.

Association of American Universities (AAU). (2005). *Non-tenure-track faculty report.* Washington, DC: Association of American Universities.

Baldwin, R. G. (1998). Technology's impact on faculty life. *New Directions for Teaching and Learning, 76,* 7–21.

Baldwin, R. G., and Chronister, J. L. (2001). *Teaching without tenure.* Baltimore: Johns Hopkins University Press.

Banachowski, G. (1996). Perspectives and perceptions: The use of part-time faculty in community colleges. *Community College Review, 42*(2), 49–62.

Bataille, G. M., and Brown, B. E. (2006). *Faculty career paths: Multiple routes to academic success and satisfaction.* Westport, CT: Praeger Publishers.

Benjamin, E. (1998). Variations in the characteristics of part-time faculty by general fields of instructional research. *New Directions for Higher Education, 104,* 45–59.

Benjamin, E. (2002). How over-reliance on non-tenure-track appointments diminishes faculty involvement in student learning. *Peer Review,* 4–10.

Benjamin, E. (Ed.). (2003a). *Exploring the role of non-tenure-track instructional staff in undergraduate learning.* San Francisco: Jossey-Bass.

Benjamin, E. (2003b). Reappraisal and implications for policy and research. *New Directions for Higher Education, 123,* 79–113.

Berry, J. (2005). *Reclaiming the ivory tower: Organizing adjuncts to change higher education.* New York: Monthly Review Press.

Bland, C., and others. (2006). The impact of appointment type on the productivity and commitment of full-time faculty in research and doctoral institutions. *Journal of Higher Education, 77*(1), 89–121.

Bok, D. (1992). Reclaiming the public trust. *Change 24*(4), 12–19.

Bowen, H. R., and Schuster, J. H. (1986). *American professors: A national resource imperiled.* New York: Oxford University Press.

Boyer, E. (1990). *Scholarship reconsidered: Priorities of the professoriate.* Trenton, NJ: Princeton University Press.

Brewster, D. (2000). The use of part-time faculty in the community college. *Inquiry, 5*(1), 66–76.

Burgan, M. (2006). *Whatever happened to the faculty?* Baltimore: Johns Hopkins University Press.

Chait, R. (2005). *Questions of tenure.* Cambridge, MA: Harvard University Press.

Chait, R., and Ford, A. T. (1982). *Beyond traditional tenure.* San Francisco: Jossey-Bass.

Chait, R., and Trower, C. (1997). *Where tenure does not reign: Colleges with contract systems* (Forum on Faculty Roles and Rewards No. 3). Washington, DC: American Association for Higher Education.

Christensen, C. (2008). The employment of part-time faculty at community colleges. *New Directions for Higher Education, 143*, 29–36.

Clarke, L. E., and Gabert, T. E. (2004). Faculty issues related to adult degree programs. *New Directions in Adult and Continuing Education, 103*, 31–40.

Cohen, A. M., and Brawer, F. B. (2008). *The American community college.* San Francisco: Jossey-Bass.

Conley, V. M., and Leslie, D. W. (2002). *Part-time instructional faculty and staff: Who they are, what they do, and what they think.* Washington, DC: National Center for Education Statistics.

Cross, J. G., and Goldenberg, E. (2002). Why hire non-tenure-track faculty? *Peer Review, 5*(1), 25–30.

Cross, J. G., and Goldenberg, E. N. (2003). How does university decision making shape the faculty? *New Directions in Higher Education, 123*, 49–59.

Cross, J. G., and Goldenberg, E. N. (2009). *Off-track profs: Nontenured teachers in higher education.* Cambridge, MA: MIT Press.

Curtis, J. (2005). *Trends in faculty status.* Washington, DC American Association of University Professors.

Curtis, J. W., and Jacobe, M. F. (2006). *AAUP non-tenure-track faculty index, 2006.* Washington, DC: American Association of University Professors.

Dobbie, D., and Robinson, I. (2008). Reorganizing higher education in the United States and Canada: The erosion of tenure and the unionization of non-tenure-track faculty. *Labor Studies Journal, 33*(117), 117–140.

Eagan, K. (2007). A national picture of part-time community college faculty: Changing trends in demographics and employment characteristics. *New Directions in Community Colleges, 140*, 5–14.

Eagan, M. K., and Jaeger, A. J. (2009). Effects of exposure to part-time faculty on community college transfer. *Research in Higher Education, 50*, 168–188.

Ehrenberg, R. G. (2005). The changing nature of the faculty and faculty employment practices. *TIAA-CREF Institute Conference "The New Balancing Act in Higher Education,"* New York, NY.

Ehrenberg, R. G., and Zhang, L. (2004). *The changing nature of faculty employment.* Retrieved May 12, 2009, from http//digitalcommons.ilr.cornell.edu/workingpapers/43.

Ehrenberg, R. G., and Zhang, L. (2005). Do tenured and tenure-track faculty matter? *Journal of Human Resources, 45*(3), 647–659.

Euben, D. *Academic freedom of professors and institutions.* (2002). Washington, DC: American Association of University Professsors Counsel.

Feldman, D. C., and Turnley, W. (2001). A field study of adjunct faculty: The impact of career stage on reactions to non-tenure-track jobs. *Journal of Career Development, 28*(1), 1–16.

Forrest Cataldi, F. E., Fahimi, M., and Bradburn, E. M. (2005). National Study of Postsecondary Faculty (NSOPF:04). Report on faculty and instructional staff in fall 2003 (NCES 2005–172). Washington, DC: U.S. Department of Education, National Center for Education Statistics. Retrieved June 1, 2010, from http://nces.ed.gov/pubsearch.

Gappa, J. (1984). *Part-time faculty: Higher education at a crossroads.* ASHE-ERIC Higher Education Report no. 3. Washington, DC: Association for the Study of Higher Education.

Gappa, J., Austin, A., and Trice, A. (2007). *Rethinking faculty work: Higher education's strategic imperative.* San Francisco: Jossey-Bass.

Gappa, J., and Leslie, D. (1993). *The invisible faculty: Improving the status of part-timers in higher education.* San Francisco: Jossey-Bass.

Hamilton, N., and Gaff, J. (Eds.). (2009). *The future of the professoriate: Academic freedom, peer review, and shared governance.* Washington, DC: Association of American Colleges and Universities.

Harper, E. P., Baldwin, R. G., Gansneder, B. G., and Chronister, J. L. (2001). Full-time women faculty off the tenure rack: Profile and practice. *Review of Higher Education, 24*(3), 237–257.

Hollenshead, C., and others. (2007). *Making the best of both worlds: Findings from a national institution-level survey on non-tenure-track faculty.* Ann Arbor, MI: Center for the Education of Women.

Jacobsohn, W. (2001). The real scandal in higher education. In E. Schell and P. Stock (Eds.), *Moving a mountain: Transforming the role of non-tenure track faculty in composition studies and higher education.* Urbana, IL: National Council of Teachers of English.

Jacoby, D. (2006). Effects of part-time faculty employment on community college graduation rates. *Journal of Higher Education, 77*(6), 1081–1102.

Jaeger, A., and Eagan, M. K. (2009). Unintended consequences: Examining the effect of part-time faculty members on associate's degree completion. *Community College Review, 36*, 167–194.

Kauffman, K. (2005). Adjunct faculty in community colleges: An academic administrator's guide to recruiting, supporting, and retaining great teachers. In D. L. Wallin (Ed.), *Adjunct faculty in community colleges,* pp. 145–160. Bolton, MA: Anker Publishing.

Kezar, A., Lester, J., and Anderson, G. (2006). Challenging stereotypes that interfere with effective governance. *Thought and Action, 42*, 121–134.

Kezar, A., and Sam, C. (2009). Institutionalizing equitable policies and practices for contingent faculty. Paper presented at a meeting of the Association for the Study of Higher Education, Vancouver, BC.

Kezar, A., and Sam, C. (2010a). Beyond Contracts: Non-tenure Track Faculty and Campus Governance. *NEA Almanac, 15,* 83–91.

Kezar, A., and Sam, C. (2010b). *Non-Tenure-Track Faculty in Higher Education: Theories and Tensions.* ASHE Higher Education Report, Vol. 36, No. 5. San Francisco: Jossey-Bass.

Leslie, D. W., Kellams, S. E., and Gunne, G. M. (1982). *Part-time faculty in American higher education.* New York: Praeger.

Levin, J. S., Kater, S., and Wagoner, R. L. (2006). *Community college faculty: At work in the new economy.* New York: Palgrave Macmillan.

Maid, B. (2001). Non-tenure-track instructors at UALR: Breaking rules, splitting departments. In E. Schell and P. Stock (Eds.), *Moving a mountain: Transforming the role of non-tenure-track faculty in composition studies and higher education*. Urbana, IL: National Council of Teachers of English.

Maynard, D. C., and Joseph, T. A. (2008). Are all part-time faculty underemployed? The influence of faculty status preference on satisfaction and commitment. *Higher Education, 55*, 139–154.

McLaughlin, F. (2005). Adjunct faculty at the community college: Second-class professoriate? *Teaching English in the Two-Year College, 33*(2), 185–193.

Monks, J. (2007). The relative earnings of non-tenure-track faculty in higher education. *Journal of Labor Research, 28*, 487–501.

National Center for Education Statistics. (2009). *Employees in postsecondary institutions, fall 2007 and salaries of full-time instructional faculty, 2007–08*. Washington, DC: U.S. Department of Education.

National Education Association. (2002). *NEA higher education policy statement on part-time and temporary faculty*. Washington, DC: National Education Association.

National Education Association Research Center. (2007). *Part-time faculty: A look at data and issues*. Washington, DC: NEA.

O'Meara, K., Terosky, A., and Neumann, A. (2008). *Faculty careers and work lives: A professional growth perspective*. San Francisco: Jossey-Bass.

Outcalt, C. (2002). *A profile of the community college professorate, 1975–2000*. New York: Routledge.

Pisani, A. M., and Stott, N. (1998). An investigation of part-time faculty commitment to developmental advising. *Research in Higher Education, 39*(2), 121–142.

Pratt, L. R. (1997). Disposable faculty: Part-time exploitation as management strategy. In C. Nelson (Ed.), *Will teach for food: Academic labor in crisis* (pp. 264–277). Minneapolis: University of Minnesota Press.

Rhoades, G. (1996). Reorganizing the faculty workforce for flexibility: Part-time professional labor. *Journal of Higher Education, 67*(6), 626–658.

Rhoades, G. (1998). *Managed professionals: Unionized faculty and restructuring academic labor*. Albany: State University of New York Press.

Rhoades, G., and Maitland, C. (2008). Bargaining for full-time non-tenure-track faculty: Best practices. *NEA 2008 Almanac of Higher Education, 13*, 67–73.

Rule, C. S. (2000). Freedom in the academy: Academic freedom explored. In Trower, C. A. (Ed.), *Policies on faculty appointment: Standard practices and unusual arrangements*. Bolton, MA: Anker Publishing.

Schell, E., and Stock, P. (2001). (Eds.). *Moving a mountain: Transforming the role of non-tenure track faculty in composition studies and higher education*. Urbana, IL: National Council of Teachers of English.

Schuster, J. H., and Finkelstein, M. J. (2006). *The American faculty: The restructuring of academic work and careers*. Baltimore: Johns Hopkins University Press.

Shaker, G. (2008). *Off the track: Full-time nontenure-track faculty experience in English*. Dissertation, Indiana University.

Shavers, F. L. (2000). Academic ranks and titles of full-time non-tenure-track faculty. In S. Slaughter and G. Rhoades (2004). *Academic capitalism and the new economy: Markets, state, and higher education*. Baltimore: Johns Hopkins University Press.

Slaughter, S., and Rhoades, E. (2004). *Academic capitalism and the new economy: Markets, state, and higher education*. Baltimore: Johns Hopkins University, Press.

Study Group on the Conditions of Excellence in Higher Education (1984). *Involvement in learning: Realizing the potential of American higher education*. Washington, DC: National Institute of Education.

Sullivan, W. (2004). *Work and integrity*. San Francisco: Jossey-Bass.

Thedwall, K. (2008). Non-tenure-track faculty: Rising numbers, lost opportunities. *New Directions for Higher Education, 143*, 11–19.

Tilly, C. (1998). Part-time work: A mobilizing issue. *New Politics, 6*(4), 21–26.

Tolbert, P. S. (1998). Two-tiered faculty systems and organizational outcomes. *New Directions for Higher Education, 104*, 71–80.

Toutkoushian, R. K., and Bellas, M. L. (2003). The effects of part-time employment and gender on faculty earnings and satisfaction: Evidence from the NSOPF:93. *Journal of Higher Education, 74*(2), 172–195.

Trower, C. A. (Ed.). (2000). *Policies on faculty appointment: Standard practices and unusual arrangements*. Bolton, MA: Anker Publishing.

Trower, C. A. (2010). How Start Over. *New York Times*. August, 12, 2010.

Tuckman, H. P. (1978). Who is part-time in academe? *AAUP Bulletin, 64*, 305–315.

Umbach, P. D. (2007). How effective are they? Exploring the impact of non-tenure-track faculty on undergraduate education. *Review of Higher Education, 30*(2), 91–123.

Wallin, D. L. (Ed.). (2005). *Adjunct faculty in community colleges*. Bolton, MA: Anker Publishing.

Winston, C. (1992). Hostility, Maximization, and the Public Trust. *Change, 24*(4), 20–27.

Wisneski, R. (2005). Investigating the research practices and library needs of non-tenure-track, tenure-track, and tenured English faculty. *Journal of Academic Librarianship, 31*(2), 119–133.

Wolf-Wendel, L., Twombly, S. B., and Rice, S. (2003). *The two-body problem: Dual-career-couple hiring policies in higher education*. Baltimore: Johns Hopkins University Press.

Wyles, B. A. (1998). Adjunct faculty in the community college: Realities and challenges. *New Directions for Higher Education, 104*, 89–93.

Name Index

A

Altbach, P., 84
Anderson, E. L., 15, 27, 69
Anderson, G., 86
Anson, C., 107
Antony, J. S., 65
Arnold, J., 68
Austin, A., 35, 36, 37, 42, 43, 63, 73, 86

B

Baldwin, R. G., 1, 2, 17, 19, 26, 28, 29, 30,
    31, 32, 34, 35, 40, 42, 43, 44, 46, 52,
    53, 54, 55, 56, 57, 58, 59, 60, 62, 63,
    64, 68, 69, 70, 71, 72, 73, 78, 81, 83,
    86, 87, 88, 89, 90, 91, 92, 93, 98, 100
Banachowski, G., 11
Bataille, G. M., 35
Bellas, M. L., 10, 54, 65, 67
Benjamin, E., 3, 30, 31, 35, 45, 46, 50, 65,
    66, 80
Berry, J., 10, 37
Bland, C., 10, 11, 85
Boyer, E., 13, 81
Bowen, H. R., 12
Bradburn, E. M., 3, 21, 22, 23, 24, 31, 42
Brawer, F. B., 26, 27
Brewster, D., 26, 27
Brown, B. E., 35
Burgan, M., 7, 31, 35, 80

C

Chait, R., 1, 10, 35, 39, 81, 82, 83, 84, 100

Christensen, C., 27
Chronister, J. L., 1, 2, 17, 19, 26, 28, 29,
    30, 31, 34, 35, 40, 42, 43, 44, 46, 52,
    53, 54, 55, 56, 57, 58, 59, 60, 62, 63,
    64, 68, 69, 70, 71, 72, 73, 78, 81, 83,
    86, 87, 88, 89, 90, 91, 92, 93, 98, 100
Clarke, L. E., 50
Cohen, A. M., 26, 27
Conley, V. M., 36, 37, 50, 53, 55, 57, 63,
    65, 73, 92
Cooper, C. L., 68
Cross, J. G., 1, 9, 10, 26, 28, 30, 31, 32,
    33, 52, 62, 83, 86, 87, 98, 101
Curtis, J. W., 3, 20, 21, 54

D

Dobbie, D., 25

E

Eagan, M. K., 11, 21, 68
Ehrenberg, R. G., 10, 25, 43
Euben, D., 73

F

Fahimi, M., 3, 21, 22, 23, 24, 31, 42
Feldman, D. C., 66
Finkelstein, M. J., 1, 2, 3, 17, 21, 22, 23, 24,
    25, 42, 43, 44, 45, 58, 63, 65, 74, 112
Ford, A. T., 1, 10, 82, 100
Forrest Cataldi, F. E., 3, 21, 22, 23, 24,
    31, 42

G

Gabert, T. E., 50
Gaff, J., 107
Gansneder, B. G., 42, 43
Gappa, J., 1, 2, 10, 12, 17, 20, 21, 26, 27,
    31, 32, 33, 34, 35, 36, 37, 40, 42, 43,
    46, 49, 50, 51, 52, 53, 54, 55, 56, 57,
    59, 60, 61, 62, 63, 68, 69, 70, 71, 72,
    73, 78, 83, 86, 87, 88, 89, 90, 91, 92,
    93, 98, 100, 101, 111
Goldenberg, E. N., 1, 10, 26, 28, 30, 31,
    32, 33, 52, 62, 83, 86, 87, 98, 101
Gunne, G. M., 13, 61, 98

H

Hamilton, N., 107
Harper, E. P., 42
Hollenshead, C., 1, 17, 25, 27, 31, 32, 33,
    35, 36, 39, 46, 47, 50, 52, 53, 54, 57,
    58, 59, 60, 63, 69, 72, 74, 86, 87, 88,
    89, 91, 105, 109

J

Jacobe, M. F., 3, 20, 21
Jacobsohn, W., 77
Jacoby, D., 11, 66
Jaeger, A., 11, 68
Jewell, R., 107
Joseph, T. A., 10, 35, 62, 65, 66, 68

K

Kater, S., 27, 34, 36
Kauffman, K., 91
Kellams, S. E., 13, 61, 98
Kezar, A., 3, 4, 9, 45, 47, 61, 62, 68, 70,
    73, 77, 79, 86, 98, 101, 112

L

Lampedusa, G. di, 107
Leslie, D. W., 1, 2, 10, 12, 17, 20, 21, 26,
    27, 31, 32, 33, 34, 35, 36, 37, 40, 42,
    43, 46, 49, 50, 51, 52, 53, 54, 55, 56,
    57, 59, 60, 61, 62, 63, 65, 68, 69, 70,
    72, 73, 78, 83, 86, 87, 88, 89, 90, 91,
    92, 93, 98, 100, 101, 111
Levin, J. S., 27, 34, 36

M

McLaughlin, F., 27
Maid, B., 49
Maitland, C., 57, 72, 88, 89, 91, 92
Maynard, D. C., 10, 35, 62, 65, 66, 68
Monks, J., 27, 32

N

Neumann, A., 10, 67, 90, 114

O

O'Meara, K., 10, 67, 90, 114
Outcalt, C., 25, 55, 63, 65, 67, 72

P

Pisani, A. M., 70
Pratt, L. R., 31

R

Rhoades, G., 10, 26, 30, 57, 72, 79, 88,
    89, 91, 92, 98, 102
Rice, S., 32, 37
Robertson, I. T., 68
Robinson, I., 25
Rule, C. S., 86

S

Sam, C., 3, 45, 47, 61, 62, 70, 73, 77, 86,
    98, 101, 112
Schell, E., 1, 13, 26, 53, 61, 81, 93, 102, 116
Schuster, J. H., 1, 2, 3, 12, 17, 21, 22, 23,
    24, 25, 43, 44, 45, 58, 65, 74, 112
Shaker, G., 64, 68, 69, 115
Shavers, F. L., 23, 37, 38
Slaughter, S., 26, 30, 79, 98
Stock, P., 1, 13, 26, 53, 61, 81, 93, 102, 116
Stott, N., 70
Sullivan, W., 88

T

Terosky, A., 10, 67, 90, 114
Thedwall, K., 26, 28
Tilly, C., 35
Tolbert, P. S., 32
Toutkoushian, R. K., 10, 54, 65, 67

Subject Index

A

"Academic capitalism," 79

Academic fields: full-time faculty differences among, 24; part-time faculty differences among, 22; research conclusions and implications for, 114–115

Academic freedom: concerns over lack of, 73; professionalizing by protecting, 92

Adjunct Advocate (journal), 14, 102

Adjunct Nation, 14, 102

Administration: faculty duties taken by, 35; non-tenure-track faculty trends by, 8

Advocacy strategies, 104–105

African American faculty, 43, 44

Alaska Natives faculty, 44

Allies: constructive use of, 105; identifying, 104–105

American Association for Higher Education (AAHE), 13

American Association of University Professors (AAUP), 14, 20, 36, 42, 60, 73, 80, 82, 98, 101

American Council on Education (ACE), 15

The American Faculty: The Restructuring of Academic Work and Careers (Schuster and Finkelstein), 1

American Federation of Teachers (AFT), 14, 17, 21, 23–24, 25, 43, 46, 50, 61, 65, 73, 81, 83, 88, 89, 90, 91, 92, 98, 102, 104

Annual Report on the Economic Status of the Profession, 2004–2205 (AAUP), 42

B

Asian faculty, 44

Asian-Pacific Islander faculty, 43, 44

Aspiring academics part-time faculty, 35

Association of American Universities (AAU), 15, 42

B

Benefits: comparison of part-time/full-time, 31–32, 54–55; professionalizing by offering equitable, 89

C

Campus climate, 105

Career enders part-time faculty, 34

Career mobility, 44–45

The Chronicle of Higher Education, 60

Coalition on the Academic Labor, 14, 110

Coalition of Contingent Academic Labor (COCAL), 102

Collective bargaining, 109

Commitment level, 67–68

Communications Workers of America, 77

Community colleges: "faculty of convenience" criticism of, 27; faculty employment patterns of, 21–22; professionalizing non-tenure-track faculty at, 96–98; rise of part-time faculty in, 26–27

Compensation: comparison of part-time/full-time, 31–32, 53–54; non-tenured faculty concerns about, 68–69; professionalizing by offering equitable, 89

Contingent track, 6
Contract renewal, 72

E

Evaluation: concerns over fairness of, 71–72; professionalizing by establishing systems of, 90; research conclusion and implications for, 111
Experts part-time faculty, 34

F

Faculty: terminology used for, 7; variety of international norms for, 84–85. *See also* Non-tenure-track faculty; Tenured faculty
Faculty appointment quotas, 80–81
Faculty degrees: non-tenure-track faculty, 45–46; tenure-track faculty, 46
Faculty Forum on Roles and Rewards of the American Association for Higher Education, 13
Freelancer part-time faculty, 35
Full-time equivalent (FTE) hours, 38, 39
Full-time non-tenure-track faculty: academic fields differences on, 24; career mobility for, 44–45; degrees and academic backgrounds, 45–46; demand for, 31–33; description of, 22–23; functional typologies of, 33–37; gender differences in, 41–43; hiring expectations for, 46–47; historical development of, 25–26, 28–31; institutional differences on, 23–24; IPEDs data on, 20–21; racial and ethnic differences, 43–44; titles of, 37–41; unionized campuses and, 25

G

Gender differences: Full-time and part-time faculty, 41–43; research conclusions and implications for, 111–112
GI bill (1944), 26
Governance: non-tenure faculty lack of participation in, 69–70; professionalize by incorporating faculty in, 91; professionalizing by facilitating participation in, 104

H

Hampshire College, 82
HERI faculty survey (UCLA), 113
Higher education: declining public support for, 29–30; factors impacting funding of, 29–30. *See also* Institutions
Higher Education Research Institute (HERI), 11
Hiring practices: professionalizing faculty by rethinking, 88–89; professionalizing faculty regularizing, 87; working conditions of, 51–53
Hispanic faculty, 43, 44
Hostile climate, 61–62
Hybrid institutions, 83–85

I

Ideology research issue, 8–9
Institutions: concerns over inconsistent faculty policies of, 70–71; corporate business model adopted for funding, 29–30; creating hybrid, 83–85; demand for non-tenure-track faculty by, 31–33; development of full-time and part-time faculty in, 25–31; full-time faculty differences among, 23–24; job responsibilities and expectations of, 57–60; new strategies for funding by, 30–31; part-time faculty differences among, 21–22; planned faculty use policies by, 78–105; research on motivation and type of, 114–115; strategies for professionalizing non-tenure-track faculty, 98–105; two-class system of tenured/non-tenured faculty, 62–64. *See also* Higher education
Integrated Postsecondary Education Data System (IPEDS), 20, 23
The Invisible Faculty: Improving the Status of Part-Timers in Higher Education (Gappa and Leslie), 17, 49

J

Job responsibilities/expectations, 57–60
Job security/seniority, 56–57, 68–69

M

Making the Best of Both Worlds (Hollenshead and others), 17

Mobilizing non-tenure-track faculty, 103

Motivation research, 114–115

N

National Center for Education Statistics (NCES), 11, 23, 42, 43

National Education Association (NEA), 14, 25, 56, 98

National Education Association Research Center, 21, 22

National Study of Postsecondary Faculty (NSOPF), 11, 24, 46, 112

Native American faculty, 42, 43, 44

New Faculty Majority (NFM), 14, 102, 110

New Pathways Project, 13

New York Times, 83

Non-tenure-track faculty: administration trends regarding, 8; definition of, 5; ensuring intentional approach to deployment of, 98–105; examining the current status of, 1–2; heterogeneous nature of, 11–12, 108–109; historical and social forces shaping, 12; planned use policies on, 78–105; professionalizing, 83, 85–98; purpose and audience of literature on, 4–5; taking a balanced approach to examining, 2–4; terminology related to, 5–8. *See also* Faculty

Non-tenure-track faculty benefits: commitment as, 67–68; satisfaction as, 65–67

Non-tenure-track faculty concerns: academic freedom as, 73; contract renewal as, 72; evaluation as, 71–72; exclusion from governance, 69–70; inconsistent policy as, 70–71; promotion as, 72–73; salary and job security, 68–69; teaching restrictions, 71; tenure-track restrictions as, 74

Non-tenure-track faculty experience: concerns and unmet expectations, 68–74; literature and research on,

49–51; perspective on faculty life and, 60–64; two-class system of tenured and, 62–64; upsides of non-tenure-track faculty work, 64–68; working conditions, 51–59

Non-Tenure-Track Faculty Index (AAUP), 20

Non-tenure-track faculty portrait: career mobility, 44–45; demand for non-tenure-track faculty, 31–33; faculty composition, 41–43; faculty degrees and academic backgrounds, 45–46; functional typologies, 33–37; hiring expectations, 46–47; historical developments, 25–31; racial and ethnic differences, 43–44; titles used for non-tenure-track faculty, 37–41; trends in part-time and full-time, 20–25

Non-Tenure-Track Faculty Report (AAU), 42

Non-tenure-track faculty research: future directions for, 112–115; heterogeneity issue of, 11–12; historical and contextual analysis issue of, 12; ideology issue of, 8–9; lack of meaningful data issue of, 10–11; overall conclusions and implications of, 108–112; stakeholders interested in, 12–16; theory issue of, 9–10

"Nonstatus appointments," 37

Nontenure track: definition of, 5, 6; other terminology used for, 6

O

Organizational theory, 10

Orientation, 53

P

Part-time non-tenure-track faculty: academic fields differences on, 22; basic salary and lack of benefits for, 31–32; career mobility for, 44–45; degrees and academic backgrounds, 45–46; demand for, 31–33; description of, 21; functional typologies of, 33–37; gender differences in, 41–43; hiring expectations for, 46–47; historical development of, 25–28; institutional differences on, 21–22; IPEDs data on, 20–21; racial and ethnic differences, 43–44; titles of, 37–41

Planned faculty use: assumptions underlying examination of, 78; broad recommendations for, 79–85; creating plan of action, 103; using data, benchmarks, and models for, 103–104; examples of professionalization of non-tenure-track faculty, 92–98; issues to consider for, 78–79; for professionalizing non-tenure-track faculty, 85–92; strategies for ensuring intentionality of non-tenure faculty, 98–105

Planned faculty use recommendations: convert to tenure track over time, 80; create hybrid institutions, 83–85; eradicate tenure and move to long-term renewable contracts, 82–83; modify tenure, 81–82; professionalize non-tenure-track faculty, 83; set tenure or faculty appointment quotas, 80–81

President's Commission on Higher Education, 26

Professional development: concerns over lack of, 55–56; professionalizing by providing, 90–91

Professionalizing non-tenure-track faculty: from the bottom up, 101–105; communicate a message of respect for, 86–87; community college example of, 96–98; creating systematic inclusion process, 87–88; defining roles clearly, 89–90; ensuring necessary resources, 92; incorporating faculty in institutional governance, 91; issues to consider for, 85–86; offering equitable compensation and benefits, 89; private research university example of, 93–95; promotion and evaluation systems, 90; protecting academic freedom, 92; providing professional development, 90–92; recommendation for, 83; regularize hiring for, 87; research conclusions and implications for, 110; from the top down, 99–101

Professionalizing strategies: address campus climate, 105; use allies, 105; create campuswide representative body for advising, 100–101; creating plan of action, 103; creating regular meeting task force or committee, 104; using data, benchmarks, and models, 103–104; develop an academic staffing plan, 99–100; garner outside pressure, 104; identify allies, 104–105; including multiple stakeholders in change process, 101; mobilizing, 103; monitor use of non-tenure-track faculty, 100; participating in governance, 104

Professionals part-time faculty, 34

Promotion career path, 72–73, 90

R

Racial/ethnic differences: part-time and full-time faculty, 43–44; research conclusions and implications for, 111–112

Recruitment and hiring, 51–53

Research and doctorate-granting universities: corporate business model for funding, 29; example of professionalizing non-tenure-track faculty at, 93–95; faculty employment patterns of, 21–22; impact of GI bill on, 26; new strategies for funding by, 30–31

Researcher faculty, 35

Resource accessibility, 92

Respect, 86–87

Role definition issue, 57–60

S

Salary: comparison of part-time/full-time, 31–32, 53–54; non-tenured faculty concerns about, 68–69; professionalizing by offering equitable, 89

Satisfaction level, 65–67

Scholarship Reconsidered: Priorities of the Professoriate (Boyer), 13, 81

Servicemen's Readjustment Act (1944) [GI bill], 26

Specialists part-time faculty, 34

About the Authors

Adrianna Kezar has been associate professor for higher education at the University of Southern California since 2003. She holds a Ph.D. and an M.A. in higher education administration from the University of Michigan. She was formerly editor of the ASHE-ERIC Higher Education Report Series from 1996 to 2004. Kezar has published more than seventy-five journal articles, fifty book chapters, and twelve books. Her research focuses on helping create meaningful changes in higher education related to diversity and equity. Recent books include: *Recognizing and Serving Low-Income Students in Higher Education* (Routledge Press), *Understanding the New Faculty Norm: Contingent Faculty in Higher Education* (Jossey-Bass), and *Enhancing Leadership Capacity on Campus: Faculty and Staff Grassroots Leadership* (Stanford Press). Kezar has also served on several editorial boards and received national awards for her work on leadership and change.

Cecile Sam is a doctoral candidate in higher education policy at the Center for Higher Education Policy Analysis at the University of Southern California. Her research interests include leadership and organization theory as applied to faculty work in higher education, with a special interest in ethics.

About the ASHE Higher Education Report Series

Since 1983, the ASHE (formerly ASHE-ERIC) Higher Education Report Series has been providing researchers, scholars, and practitioners with timely and substantive information on the critical issues facing higher education. Each monograph presents a definitive analysis of a higher education problem or issue, based on a thorough synthesis of significant literature and institutional experiences. Topics range from planning to diversity and multiculturalism, to performance indicators, to curricular innovations. The mission of the Series is to link the best of higher education research and practice to inform decision making and policy. The reports connect conventional wisdom with research and are designed to help busy individuals keep up with the higher education literature. Authors are scholars and practitioners in the academic community. Each report includes an executive summary, review of the pertinent literature, descriptions of effective educational practices, and a summary of key issues to keep in mind to improve educational policies and practice.

The Series is one of the most peer reviewed in higher education. A National Advisory Board made up of ASHE members reviews proposals. A National Review Board of ASHE scholars and practitioners reviews completed manuscripts. Six monographs are published each year and they are approximately 120 pages in length. The reports are widely disseminated through Jossey-Bass and John Wiley & Sons, and they are available online to subscribing institutions through Wiley InterScience (http://www.interscience.wiley.com).

Call for Proposals

The ASHE Higher Education Report Series is actively looking for proposals. We encourage you to contact one of the editors, Dr. Kelly Ward (kaward@wsu.edu) or Dr. Lisa Wolf-Wendel (lwolf@ku.edu), with your ideas.

The Global Growth of Private Higher Education

Recent Titles

ASHE HIGHER EDUCATION REPORT
ORDER FORM SUBSCRIPTION AND SINGLE ISSUES

DISCOUNTED BACK ISSUES:

Use this form to receive 20% off all back issues of *ASHE Higher Education Report*.
All single issues priced at **$23.20** (normally $29.00)

TITLE	ISSUE NO.	ISBN

Call 888-378-2537 or see mailing instructions below. When calling, mention the promotional code JBNND to receive your discount. For a complete list of issues, please visit www.josseybass.com/go/aehe

SUBSCRIPTIONS: (1 YEAR, 6 ISSUES)

☐ New Order   ☐ Renewal

U.S.	☐ Individual: $174	☐ Institutional: $265
CANADA/MEXICO	☐ Individual: $174	☐ Institutional: $325
ALL OTHERS	☐ Individual: $210	☐ Institutional: $376

Call 888-378-2537 or see mailing and pricing instructions below.
Online subscriptions are available at www.onlinelibrary.wiley.com

ORDER TOTALS:

Issue / Subscription Amount: $ _____

Shipping Amount: $ _____
(for single issues only – subscription prices include shipping)

Total Amount: $ _____

SHIPPING CHARGES:

First Item	$5.00
Each Add'l Item	$3.00

(No sales tax for U.S. subscriptions. Canadian residents, add GST for subscription orders. Individual rate subscriptions must be paid by personal check or credit card. Individual rate subscriptions may not be resold as library copies.)

BILLING & SHIPPING INFORMATION:

☐ **PAYMENT ENCLOSED:** *(U.S. check or money order only. All payments must be in U.S. dollars.)*

☐ **CREDIT CARD:**   ☐ VISA   ☐ MC   ☐ AMEX

Card number _____ Exp. Date _____

Card Holder Name _____ Card Issue # _____

Signature _____ Day Phone _____

☐ **BILL ME:** *(U.S. institutional orders only. Purchase order required.)*

Purchase order # _____
Federal Tax ID 13559302 • GST 89102-8052

Name _____

Address _____

Phone _____ E-mail _____

Copy or detach page and send to: **John Wiley & Sons, PTSC, 5th Floor**
989 Market Street, San Francisco, CA 94103-1741

Order Form can also be faxed to: **888-481-2665**

PROMO JBNND